643.2 Fenwick, Daman C.
FEN
Cop. 1 Mobile home living

DATE			
APR 2 7 2004			

Danville Public Library
Danville, Illinois

© THE BAKER & TAYLOR CO.

No. 1322
$14.95

MOBILE HOME LIVING:
The Money-Saving Guide
BY DAMAN C. FENWICK

TAB TAB BOOKS Inc.
BLUE RIDGE SUMMIT, PA. 17214

FIRST EDITION

FIRST PRINTING

JANUARY—1981

Copyright © 1981 by TAB BOOKS Inc.

Printed in the United States of America

Reproduction or publication of the content in any manner, without express
permission of the publisher, is prohibited. No liability is assumed with respect to
the use of the information herein.

Library of Congress Cataloging in Publication Data

Fenwick, Daman C
   Mobile home living.

     Includex index.
     1. Mobile home living. I. Title
TX1105.F46   1980   643'.2   80-21441
ISBN 0-8306-9670-9
g m 0-8306-1322-6 (pbk.)

Contents

Danville Public Library
Danville, Illinois

Preface

Some clown is always asking me, "Why do you live in a trailer?" It's a silly question and it irritates me. To save money, of course. If I didn't have to worry about money, I'd rent the top ten floors of Waldorf Towers, with my own helicopter pad and ten Playboy Bunnies to rub my aching back.

I worry about money, so I live in a mobile home—not a trailer—and answer more silly questions every Sunday afternoon when an invading horde of house hunters comes driving through my park. Sometimes I hide in my workshop. Sometimes they sneak up, catch me unawares, and ask directions to the office. Then they hang around, asking endless questions, like "How do you keep your pipes from freezing?" "How do you keep out mice?" "How do you like living in a trailer?"

That last touches a tender nerve and irritates me to the point that I abruptly end the questions-and-answers with, "I wouldn't know. I've never *lived* in a trailer."

That's true. A trailer is something you hitch to the back of a car and pull up to some lake for a weekend of fishing. A mobile home is not mobile. Some of them are harder to move than the pyramids of Giza.

So, besides saving money, is there any other reason why I live in a mobile home?

Yes. I like them.

Then how come there are so many disenchanted people complaining about living in "aluminum ghettos?" How come there's so much bad press? How come there's so many investigations of the industry?

There are three reasons.

(a) Because there are all kinds of people in the world: winners, losers, frustrated bank tellers, little old ladies, to name only a few. They all live out their lives in "quiet desperation," as Thoreau once said.

(b) Because, as an officer of the Minnesota Mobile Homeowner's Protective Association told a state senate committee, "There's absolutely nothing wrong with mobile homes that couldn't be easily corrected with a few public lynchings, the bodies left swaying in the breeze."

(c) Because, as Jimmy Durante used to say, "Dem's the conditions that prevail."

The late Showman Billy Rose, a shrewd man with a dollar, once said, "Never invest your money in anything that eats or has to be painted." For this reason, mobile homes are a good investment—but not for people like Preston, a stubborn, dedicated man of principle who recently bought a magnificent home in my park.

Lou Holz, famed raconteur, used to tell a funny story about an uncle of his who was also a stubborn man of principle. The uncle had gone to a dentist with a throbbing toothache. When the dentist asked which tooth ached, the uncle said, "You got the education, *you* find out!"

So the dentist pulled a tooth. It was the wrong one. Again he asked which tooth ached. Again the uncle replied, "You got the education. You find out."

This went on with the dentist pulling tooth after tooth until only one remained. "And you know," Lou Holz said, "that was ten years ago—and my uncle's tooth *still* aches!"

That is exactly what happened to Preston the first day in his new home when he and his friends were startled by a scream coming from the bathroom. Rushing back to investigate, they could barely see Preston's wife, Clara, holding up her skirt, almost completely enveloped in steam. It seems that when she flushed the toilet the second time, steam came out.

It was no big deal, really. Somebody at the factory had goofed in the final coupling of the copper water lines and crossed the hot to the cold side. In mobile home plumbing, this is an easy mistake to make—and an easy one to correct. It only takes a few minutes with an adjustable wrench. However, when a neighbor offered to switch the pipes, Preston drew himself up haughtily.

"No! Leave it alone! The factory made the mistake. Let *them* fix it!"

Well, that was three months ago; steam is still coming out of that toilet. Preston, a stubborn man of great principle, is having chest pains. Clara is close to a nervous breakdown. Lawyers are exchanging letters with other lawyers because Clara suffered shock, embarrassment, and mental suffering.

Preston is a dedicated loser. History tells us that stubborn men of great principle, like Thomas Moore and Becket, always end up getting hit in the neck with an ax. There are thousands of other Prestons all over the country in mobile home communities, eating their hearts out in bitter frustration because something or other won't work, something is loose, something leaks, or something sticks. And all they do is complain endlessly, write letters to newspaper "Zip Lines," congressmen, and consumer groups.

Now, let's look at a winner, Charlie, who also lives in my park. On the first night in their new custom-built mobile home, Charlie's wife complained that the master bedroom ceiling light wouldn't work. Charlie made all the obvious checks, but could find nothing wrong. Then he removed the cover plate on the wall switch—and *there* was the trouble. The switch had been installed upside down. Charlie had specified silent mercury switches, which will not work in the upside down position because fluid mercury in a small glass vial makes the electrical connection.

And again somebody on the assembly line goofed, just like they goof on Detroit auto assembly lines, even in the building of expensive homes by private contractors of the highest reputation. (A 7 million dollar goof was made in Boston on the 62-story John Hancock Tower when 10,300 windows had to be replaced.) Goofs, no matter what the cost, are not the end of the world. But how a person reacts, or over-reacts, is what marks the difference between a loser and a winner. This is how a winner reacted when a light switch wouldn't work.

Charlie went to the refrigerator, got a can of beer, came back, and glared at the upside down mercury switch. Between sips of beer, he swore under his breath. This made him feel much better. Then he asked his wife, "Where's my tool box?"

She said, "It's gone."

"Where?"

"I sold all your tools at the garage sale."

"Now why did you do a dumb thing like that?"

"You told me to. You said you would never need tools again in a mobile home. You said it was care-free living with no maintenance, no grass cutting, no snow shoveling..."

Charlie was already out the door and on his way to Sears. He came back two hours later with his car trunk filled with new tools. Then, as he told friends later, "I fixed that damn switch."

Every mobile home community has its Prestons and its Charlies. The Prestons are bitter critics of mobile homes. The Charlies swear they never had it so good. But the great majority are frustrated in-betweens, living out their lives in "quiet desperation" because they don't know what to *do*.

This book is intended for those "in-betweens." The Prestons will never fix anything because they are men of great principle. The Charlies already fix everything and have no need for this book. The rest would like to fix things but lack the know-how and courage to tackle something out of their line.

The bank manager is frightened by anything electrical. The tough little widow, who lives alone and operates a million dollar computer at Chrysler, is intimidated by a furnace pilot light. An engineer at a 50 million dollar nuclear power installation is afraid to put up an awning by himself. A tugboat skipper, who pushes around huge ore boats, is afraid to move his mobile home.

All that these people need is courage. But, as the Wizard of Oz told the cowardly lion after pinning a hero medal on his chest, "You always had courage, you just needed a medal to prove it."

This book is your medal. To all mobile homers, with love.

Daman Fenwick

Save in
the Right Home

1

The first time I saw a man who lived in a mobile home, he was out in the middle of Lake Erie walking on water like Jesus. It was 10 miles out, almost due north from the summer resort community of Port Clinton, Ohio, which is east of Toledo, west of Cleveland. We were on vacation. It was July 24th, my eighth birthday. My father had taken me on a charter boat to troll for pickerel. *That's* when it happened!

There was a heavy summer mist and the lake surface was quiet, almost like glass. Then suddenly, through the mist off the starboard bow, we saw *him*. A woman screamed. Startled, I slipped on an orange peel and hit my chin on the top edge of a garbage can filled with ice for fish. I still have the scar. But I felt no pain as I stared at the man out there in the lake. He was actually standing *on the water*! Then he stretched out his arms and looked up into the sky.

At this point the charter boat captain slowed down the noisy engines so we could hear him as he spoke through a small megaphone. "Take it easy, folks. Back! Back! Don't crowd that starboard rail!"

The boat was listing badly, but nobody moved back. Then the captain said, "C'mon, folks! He's not really walking on water. Look at his feet. He's standing on a flat rock surface, which is the highest point of Niagara Reef, and today barely covered by water. Whenever the weather and water level conditions are just right, he comes out here in an outboard and runs it right up on that flat rocky surface. You can't see his small boat, back about 20 feet, because of the fog."

"What's he doing?" somebody asked.

"Who is he?"

"Nobody knows. They call him Hallelujah Harry. He came here about eight years ago pulling a big house trailer behind an old jalopy with Tennessee license plates. The old car broke down, so he just stayed and opened up a soul-saving mission, There's rumors that he's a defrocked minister."

"Where does he live?" some woman asked.

"In that same old house trailer . . . "

"House trailer!" the woman repeated with a knowing smile. Then she nodded and made a circular motion with a finger near her temple. There were more nods and more knowing smiles. And I immediately got the impression that anybody who lived in a house trailer was a nut.

And *that* is how prejudice took form in the mind of an 8-year-old boy. As I grew older, I became convinced that house trailers, as they were then called, were suitable only for senile old people in places like Florida, or for traveling construction workers. Anybody else who lived in a house trailer was, I thought, either a gypsy or a nut.

Many years later, I was eating breakfast one Sunday morning, deeply absorbed in the sports page, when my wife said, "It's a beautiful day. Let's go look at some mobile homes."

And I said "You're nuts."

She slapped my paper down. "What do you mean I'm nuts?"

"Who said you were?"

"You did."

"It must have been a reflex action."

"Why?"

So I told here about Hallelujah Harry, and she said, "You've been mentally conditioned against mobile homes. That's bad."

"Why?"

"You're prejudiced. Your mind is made up before you even look."

"Why do I have to look?"

"It's your business to write about ways to save money. Three faculty members of Toledo University seem to think you can in a mobile home."

"What did they say?"

"Nothing, they just bought mobile homes."

"Who are these nuts?"

She told me their names and I recognized one. Milton J., an assistant in biology. Since, as my wife said, investigative reporting is my business, I called him.

He said, "We bought one of the first homes after the first half of the park was finished. It was once a hog farm. When the wind is right, we can still smell pigs. Nobody was living there whom we could go to for free advice. They took us in all right."

"How?"

"They sold us a $30,000 aluminum Taj Mahal that we can't move or sell without losing half of our investment."

"Don't you like it?"

"We love it."

"Why would you want to move it?"

"To get away from the Sunday afternoon pests."

"What pests?"

"Sightseers who drive through the park every Sunday. If they see me outside, they stop and try to pump me for free advice. Hell, nobody gave us any free advice. Why should I let somebody else profit from my mistakes? Someday I'll write a book . . . "

I know somebody at the Chamber of Commerce. I called him at his home. He said, "There's insurance money in that park. Insurance companies are the shrewdest investors of money. Not one dollar leaves their vaults until an army of consultants, lawyers, engineers, and computers complete long range studies in depth. So they must believe in the future of mobile homes. In fact, 97 per cent of all homes sold in the United States for less than $20,000 are mobile homes. The U.S. Department of Commerce is projecting figures like 50 million Americans living in mobile homes by 1980."

This new park where the TU faculty members had bought homes is in a suburban area about 25 miles from Toledo. It has a massively impressive entrance and sign with rustic wood letters reading BLOSSOM HEATH ESTATE. (This very closely approximates the real name of this park which I will not use for reasons of honesty. This book is intended to be factual, honest, and revealing. Using real names, this would be almost impossible to do because most of the people who live in mobile homes are fearful and insecure. And so are the manufacturers and park owners. In fact, everybody in the mobile home world is afraid of something. The manufacturers and park owners have a deadly fear of reprisals from management if they make waves. No one would speak to me, not even friends, until I promised their names would not be used. I am the only mobile home owner whose identity is revealed in this book, and *I* will probably live to regret it.)

THE MOBILE HOME "SELLORAMA"

I had to slow down as I turned into the park because there were cars ahead of me. In fact, it looked like we had got caught in a funeral cortege.

My wife said, "This park has a full page ad in Sunday's paper. They're having a Sellorama today, with free donuts, hotdogs, and refreshments."

It was more like a carnival than a sale of homes. A refreshment tent was set up on one of the vacant lots. A sound system was blaring country & western music between sales spiels I wanted to leave, but we were trapped, so I just followed the line of cars until I saw an opening down a side street which wasn't too crowded.

All of the homes on this street had fluttering colored pennants and signs in the windows reading "Model Home," or "Ask about Model 12." They were all much larger than the house trailers I remembered. The bottom areas were all enclosed by aluminum panels, there were no wheels to be seen anywhere, and no hitches. One home had apparently just arrived because we could see deep tire tracks in the soft ground, but the hitch had already been removed and was lying on the ground under the home. Some of the homes had a box-like addition on one side, and one home even looked like a white Cape Cod cottage, at least 24 feet wide. I was amazed because there were no visible signs that it had been put together.

The street was crowded with children holding bottles of pop. Adults were walking back and forth, in and out of homes (Fig. 1-1). Nobody stayed in one home long because there were so many more streets, so many more homes to see. I wondered if anybody stopped to buy one.

We got out of the car, and immediately an attractive long-legged young woman in a striped T-shirt and hot pants came towards us. There was a huge white button pinned on her shirt that read "Hi, I'm Cathy." She smiled prettily and asked, "Are you folks interested in a mobile home?"

I was amazed. "Are you a salesman—I mean salewoman?"

"One of them. You look surprised."

"I am."

"We have male salesmen. Would you rather one of them showed you . . . "

"No. My wife just wanted a donut."

She smiled and shook her head. "Your wife wants to see mobile homes."

Fig. 1-1. A mobile home "sellorama" is like a game to see who can eat the most donuts and walk through the most homes without getting cornered by one of the pretty long-legged sales girls in hot pants and striped T-shirts.

"How do you know?"

"By the way you act."

"How's that?"

"When you parked your car, you just sat there a few minutes and looked around with the eyes of a hunger."

"What do other people do?"

"They jump out of their cars, slam the doors and send their kids over to the tent while they run from home to home as if they had a schedule to make."

"Don't any of them ever stop running and buy?"

She shook her head.

"Then who does?"

"People like you."

Again I was amazed. "You're so young. Where did you learn all that?"

"The organization in charge of the selling program here is Community Developers, Inc. They've got more motivational experts than paper clips. They teach us how to evaluate consumer response to advertising and pick out the serious hunter in a mob of lookers. I watched you as you turned the corner, so slow, so deliberate—like a hunter stalking. You came here today for a reason."

I frowned. "Well, this is one your motivational experts blew. We have no intentions of buying anything, today or any other day. We're just looking. A friend of mine at TU bought a home here, so we just came out to see what made him flip his lid."

A Mona Lisa smile played on her lips. "I'll be glad to show you around."

"You'll just be wasting your time," I said quickly. "I'm warning you, we're not buying."

"I know," she said. "But I'd still like to show you around."

"No obligation?"

"No obligation. And if your wife really wants a donut . . . "

"No, thanks," my wife said.

"I can tell you have some questions you want to ask."

"How did you know?"

She just shrugged with that Mona Lisa smile again.

EXPANDOS AND TIPOUTS

I pointed to a big home on the next street. "What's that box-like addition sticking out the side—and that little thing on the back (Fig. 1-2)?"

You mean the green and white Marlette? That is an 8 × 14 expando. It is called that because it expands a basic 12 × 14 living room until it becomes a more respectable 20 × 14 room. Yet, for shipping or moving purposes, the expando is easily pushed back into the living room like a dresser drawer. It pulls out the same way and sits on its own foundation of blocks, which you can't see because of the skirting.

"That addition in the back is called a tipout. It serves the same purpose as the expando on a smaller scale. The tipout does not, however, push in or out. It tips, or swings down because it is fastened to the floor on a continuous hinge. That particular tipout, which you see only on Marlette Homes, adds three feet to the length, making it a 73 footer instead of the maximum 70.

"Tipouts are more commonly on the sides of mobile homes, where they add space to living rooms (Fig. 1-3). You can tell a tipout by its roof. Note how it is angled so it will clear when it swings down into the living room. The expando roof is always flat, same as the tag roof."

"What's a tag?" my wife asked.

TAG-ALONGS

We walked down the street a way where she pointed out another new home. "We just put this one together this week. That

14

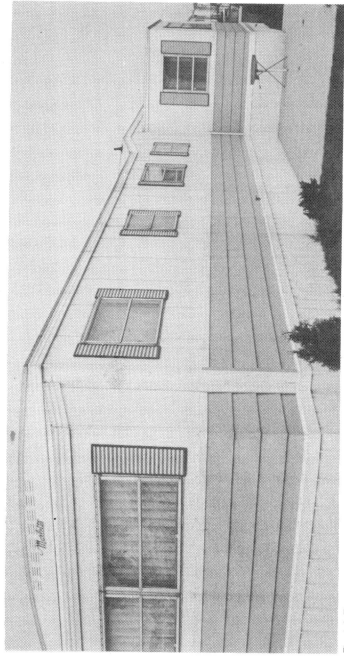

Fig. 1-2. The boxy addition sticking out the side of this mobile home expands the basic 12' by 14' living room until it becomes 20' by 14'. It is called an "expando." The extension in the back (foreground) is called a "tipout" because it tips in and out of the back bedroom on a continuous hinge. Note the slanted roof of the "tipout."

Fig. 1-3. The tipout has a continuous hinge on the bottom where it is fastened to the floor of the main structure. For shipping or moving it can be swung down into the living room. You can tell the tipout by its slanted roof, which enables it to clear when it is tipped down into the room.

half with the porch is called a tag because, as you can see, it has its own hitch and wheels. When shipped, it tags along behind the main home. That's how it got the name, tag-along, or tag for short. This particular tag (Fig. 1-4) is 60 × 14, almost the same size as the basic home to the right, which is 70 × 14. This provides 1800 square feet of living space with two full baths, three bedrooms, a big family room, big kitchen and dining area, separate utility room with washer and dryer, and a huge 28 × 14 living room. This home is complete and beautifully furnished. There is nothing else to buy. If you try to buy this much livability in a conventional home, you will wind up with a $65,000 mortgage and 35 years of payments. You can own this home with only an $18,000 mortgage and up to 12 years of payments. Just think, in 10 or 12 years you'll be free and clear while your friends still have 25 years to do on those big monthly payments and ever increasing real estate taxes."

"Hey, taxes!" I said quickly. "What kind of *taxes* do you pay on these things?"

"In this county there's a house trailer tax which you pay once a year in January. The tax is computed at 80 per cent of the total

16

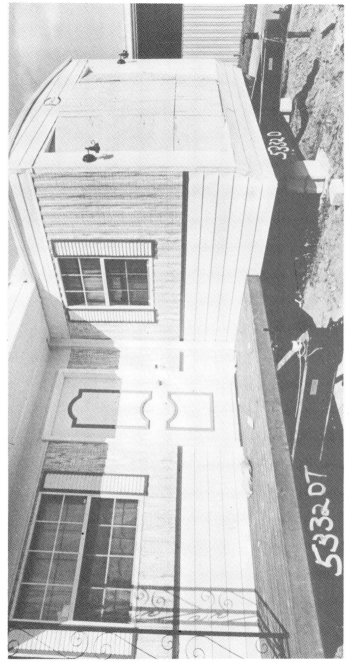

Fig. 1-4. The main home to the right, and the tag to the left, are separate units, each with its own hitch and wheel assembly. The unit to the left usually arrives a day to a week after the main home is set up, but sometimes it tags along right behind, which is how it got its name.

17

Fig. 1-5. Here is a double, as it is shipped from the factory. These two sections, when put together, will make a 65' by 24' dwelling that will look very much like a conventional home. But, at this stage they look horrible and sales people don't like to show them.

purchase price. For example, on a $10,000 home, $8,000 is the starting figure. You take 40 per cent of $8,000 to arrive at $3200. This is the figure on which your tax is computed. This tax varies in each township. In this particular township, the rate is $46.70 per thousand of valuation. That figures out at a first year tax bill of $149.44. There is a 5 per cent depreciation drop each year until 35 per cent is reached, which then becomes your permanent tax valuation."

My wife's eyes were starting to glow, so I quickly changed the subject. "How do you get those two halves together?"

"Our own set-up crew has special hydraulic equipment for just that job. The main home is first foundationed and strapped down. The tag is rolled in as close as they can get. Then the hydraulic equipment raises one end of the tag and moves it sideways, forwards or backwards, until it is in exactly the right position to be bolted together at top and bottom. All the tags and doubles are put together with that special equipment, which costs a fortune."

"What's a double?"

DOUBLES

"Two complete sections like those two over there." She pointed out two black plastic covered (Fig. 1-5) halves sitting desolately in an open area.

Fig. 1-6. The two ugly black plastic covered sections will look like this when joined. The "double" thus formed has almost 1600 square feet of living space. Few people would ever think of calling this a "trailer."

"Man, they sure look terrible in that stage," I said.

"We only have one finished double in the park at the moment, and people are living in it, so I can't show you how they look inside. But I can show you the outside. That white home over there is a double (Fig. 1.6).

"It doesn't look like a mobile home," my wife said.

"It isn't supposed to. That's what they're doing now, making them look more and more like conventional homes. In California they're designing exciting new concepts in mobile living. There's no limit to what you can do with a double. In a straight, all you get is an aluminum box—crackerbox, some call them."

"What's a straight? my wife asked.

SINGLE WIDES

"Just a single wide mobile home with nothing added on to make more room. They are what so many people still refer to as trailers. They are also the favorite with young marrieds (Fig. 1-7) because they can be bought for as little as $600 during clearance sales. Older couples walk through them, but rarely ever buy one. Our most expensive straight at the moment is $11,500. But we have a 14-wide Holly Park coming in next week that will sell for almost $13,000. It will be a lot of living space."

14-WIDES

"What's so special about a 14 wide?" I asked.

"Just getting one is special."

"Why?"

"Many states just won't issue the permits for transporting them. This state will, but the Ohio Turnpike still bans them."

"Why?"

"It's a tight squeeze for them clear the toll gates. They also have trouble maneuvering those curves on the exits."

"Then how do they get here?"

"Over state and county roads. It takes longer and costs more."

"Why?"

"There must be an additional car driving on ahead with a warning sign reading WIDE LOAD COMING. They cannot be transported on weekends, at night, or any time when heavy traffic is anticipated, like on Friday before a big football game—Ohio State and Michigan for example.

"The 70 × 12 single wide is still the most popular and basic mobile home because it's the easiest to buy and the easiest to

Fig. 1-7. Single wides are still the biggest sellers and the favorites of young marrieds, like this couple who eventually bought "Model 15" during a clearance sale. Older couples still walk through them, but rarely ever buy one.

move. Some day mobile homes will be delivered and set down on their foundations by helicopter, and there will be no limit on width."

An elderly couple had just come out of a home and beckoned to her. Cathy excused herself. As she talked to them, I noticed two other young women down the street dressed in the same manner with big white buttons on their striped T-shirts. I wondered if this was a Freudian device of the consumer motivational experts. It hardly seemed like a way to sell mobile homes, since wives have a great deal to say about such thing, and they are *not* motivated by pretty, long-legged girls in hot pants. They might be even alienated if they caught their husbands' eyes wandering. I wondered how my wife felt, so I said, "Let's blow this firetrap."

She said, "We haven't seen anything yet."

"What else is there to see?"

"The inside of a mobile home."

"Why?"

"That's where you live."

"Don't these hot pants sales girls irritate you?"

"No. Do they irritate you?"

"No."

"Then what's the problem?"

"I don't know."

"That's what I thought."

Cathy finally came back. She said, "That old couple has been here since noon. They're very anxious to buy a mobile home, but I don't think they'll ever make it. They live in that Reynolds Road area and just got hit with a $15,000 sanitary sewer assessment. When you get an assessment bill, you've got exactly 30 days to pay up in full. This couple couldn't so they just got another bill with $8,000 interest added on to the original $15,000 for 20 years. But here's the dirty part, if they were to pay off that $15,000 assessment tomorrow, they still would have to pay that $8,000 interest for only being one week late. That's why they're so mad and looking at mobile homes. But they still have to sell their house—and who would buy it with that assessment, unless there's oil under it?"

ASSESSMENTS AND REAL ESTATE TAXES

"Do mobile homes ever get assessed?" I asked.

"Not directly. It's only the owner of the land who pays real estate taxes and assessments for sewers and improvements like streets and sidewalks. Of course, a tenant pays those taxes through his rent, just as he would when renting an apartment or house in the city. Now, in some states, mobile homes are taxed just like real estate. In states where they are not taxed as real estate, like Ohio for example, you are required to pay a license tag fee. California and Florida, which are the two biggest mobile home states, have a graduated tax structure, which is computed on price and size of the home. By the way, have you ever been hit with an assessment?"

"You mean like for a sanitary sewer?"

"I mean for anything."

"Well, our street was paved eight years ago. We still owe about $400."

She gave me a wet-lipped smiled. "Then you're in pretty good shape."

"Yeah," I said. I wondered if she lived in a mobile home. I wondered if she was married. When I asked, she sighed prettily.

"Not yet. But when I do get married, I'm going to live in a mobile home. Why do you ask?"

"I thought maybe you sales people were required to live in one of these homes."

"Of course not."

"You want to live in one of these things? You're so young."

"What's being young got to do with it?"

"Well, image for one thing. Mobile homes are identified with old people, with retirement, fishing, Medicare and shuffleboard in Florida—"

"Not any more. Look around. How many old people do you see? These are mostly over-thirty-in-the-middle-years-solid-citizen types and young marrieds either living with their parents, or in expensive rented apartments which they can't afford. They finally ask one day, why collect $300-a-month rent receipts when we can live in our own home for $150-a-month—including house payment and lot rental."

FINANCING

"How did you arrive at those figures?" I asked.

"Commercial Credit Corporation specializes in mobile home financing. Here is one of their financing arrangements for a basic single wide costing $6,000. After a 20 per cent down payment of $1,200, we have $4,800. To this we add comprehensive insurance for the full period of the loan, which comes to $377. The amount to be financed is now $5,177. Mobile homes can be financed for up to 12 years, but we'll just figure this one out over 7 years with 84 payments of $95 a month. The lot rentals in this park are $60 a month. That includes water, sewer and garbage collection. It also includes grass cutting in the summer and snow removal in the winter. Of course, utility charges like electricity, telephone and heat are extra. Here we have natural gas, but in some rural areas they use LP gas or propane, which is quite expensive."

I was skeptical. "With a $6000 home, aren't there other expenses? How about those concrete steps?"

PACKAGE DEALS AND OPTIONS

"They are part of the package when you buy a home in this park. You get two concrete steps with black iron railing. You get complete skirting to match your home."

"What's skirting?" my wife asked.

"That aluminum paneling around the bottom of the home. It keeps out dogs and cats, helps keep the heat bill down, and dresses up the park by concealing all the sewer pipes and plumbing. Now, you also get a 7 × 9 steel utility building, a gas post lantern in front of your home, a completely sodded lawn of Kentucky Merion Bluegrass, two trees, one evergreen and six shrubs in front of the home. You actually don't *need* anything else. However, an optional 10 × 10 utility building is available, and so is a third concrete step."

She stopped abruptly and peered into my face. "Have you ever been *in* a mobile home?"

"Nope."

She pointed to a huge thing with eight wheels, the hitch jacked up on a cement block. There was mud splattered all over the sides. The ground was deeply rutted by the tractor that had moved it into place. "What do you think of *that?*"

I shrugged. "It just looks like a very big house trailer."

"That is *not* a house trailer!" she cut in sharply. "That is 70 feet long with an 8 × 12 expando. It weighs over 10 tons. Could you pull *that* with your car?"

"Nope."

"Then why did you call it a trailer?"

"I don't know. Is that 70 feet outside or inside?"

"It's 70 feet including the hitch. The hitch is about three feet. That makes the home actually a 67 × 12—and it's really a full 12 feet wide."

"Then why do they call it 70 × 12?"

"I don't know. Maybe for the same reason that a 2 × 4 is called a 2 × 4 when everybody know that it isn't. Now I suppose you want to know if the expando seams ever leak."

"Yeah."

"They do."

I was taken aback by her frankness. "What happens then?"

"If it's in warranty, it's fixed."

"By who?"

"The park set-up crew handles some warranty problems. Croydon Homes, one of our big sellers, has a service truck which comes here once a month to handle all accumulated problems."

"*Once a month!*" I gasped.

"We think that's pretty good. Remember now, the factories where these are built are not just around the corner. You can't expect them to rush a service truck hundreds of miles every day to fix a sticking door or . . . "

"*A leak in the roof*—you can't *wait* a month!"

"Why not," she said very calmly. "It doesn't rain every day."

"I know, I know! And the roof only leaks when it rains. But suppose I don't *want* to wait a month?"

Again she said very calmly, "You go up on the roof and fix it yourself."

"Just like that."

"Just like that," she repeated.

Her frankness disarmed me. Suddenly I liked her. Had she been evasive, like most salesmen in a similar situation, I would have questioned everything she said. I could see that my wife, Wanda, felt the same way. So I said, "Let's look at some homes."

We followed her across the street and into a brown and cream Croydon. "This is a 70 × 12 with an 8 × 12 expando, or roll-out as Croydon calls it."

My wife and I stood in that living room and sucked in our breaths as if ice water had been thrown in our faces. We were stunned! Perhaps it was the abruptness, the sudden change from the uninteresting drabness of the outside to the oppulent luxury of the inside. There is no warning. You are like Alice stepping through a mirror into Wonderland.

On the outside, most mobile homes look like long boxes covered with aluminum siding. They are definitely not an impressive sight. But beware of the interiors. *That's* where they get you. Wanda and I just stood in that surprisingly big living room and stared while off in the distance Cathy was talking about various decors in Moorish, Old English, Colonial, and Mediterranean.

The expando, or roll-out, or tip-out which protudes so gracelessly on the outside, makes a fantastic difference on the *inside*. You can see what it does to a 15 × 12 living room by looking at the floor plan drawings (Fig. 1-8.) The living room is expanded to 20 × 15. With a tip-out it is expanded to 18'7" × 17.

We were in Moorish decor because everything was black. All the walls throughout the home were richly paneled in black wood. A black wood railing separated the sunken living room from the kitchen. Thick tomato-red rugs (wall-to-wall) were in every room—even the bathroom and closets. There was a Picasso print (from his Cubist period) on the living room wall. There was a statuette bust of Egyptian Queen Nefertiti on an end table.

The furniture, black and gold, absolutely belonged in that living room. To have removed one piece would have been like lifting a bar of Beethoven's Fifth Symphony. It was the same in the kitchen, equipped with all those fascinating built-ins and appliances no woman can resist.

Suddenly all the things I had heard about "house trailers," all the prejudices instilled in my subconscious by years of looking at shabby trailer parks began to melt away like snow on a warm day in April. And my poor wife, Wanda, didn't have a chance. She was walking around in a daze, giving little shrieks when ever some new magic came to view. She would call to me, "Hey look at *this*!"

I know now, in retrospect, that we had been victimized by fiendishly clever merchandising tricks.

That Mona Lisa smile was on Cathy's lips again as she very smoothly maneuvered us into another home. She said, "This is a Landola."

"What's a Landola?"

"A Cadillac among mobile homes."

THE BEST MOBILE HOMES

"You mean this is the best?"

"Well, one of them. In mobile homes, we have Cadillacs, Lincolns, and Chrysler Imperials."

"Who are they?"

"I would say Kroft, Landola, Holly Park, and Croydon."

"Just four?"

"In this section of the country, yes."

"How come?"

"The manufacture of mobile homes is aimed at a specific market and area of the country, and they are built close to that area. Homes designed for California, Florida, and Arizona are different than homes built for the midwest, and good ones are expensive. In California, a top quality luxury home like the Viking starts at $15,000 and goes up to $50,000 and over. You might call it the Mercedes-Benz of mobile homes. The Tropicana, distributed in Florida, also goes up to $50,000 and over. Other quality homes in the south are Townhouse, Peachtree Housing, and Homes By Fisher. In the east there are Vindale, Salem House, and Deluxe Homes. None of them are cheap. You don't really need a list of names. You can pretty well rate homes yourself by their price tags. A $6,000 home is a $6,000 home regardless of who makes it. Let's face it, how much quality can you get into a home for that kind of money? By the same reasoning, when you get up over $20,000, you find quality with any brand name. Nobody can give you both quality and low price. It's as simple as that."

We went through the Landola and, as Cathy said, it was a Cadillac and had a Cadillac price tag. It had a 35 foot tag (Fig. 1-9) and it was *huge*.

CUSTOM BUILTS

Cathy said, "This Landola was custom built to the buyer's own specifications. He was a retired minister and died before it was completed. We have it on consignment to sell for the widow. You will note that the home has a classic English rectory motif."

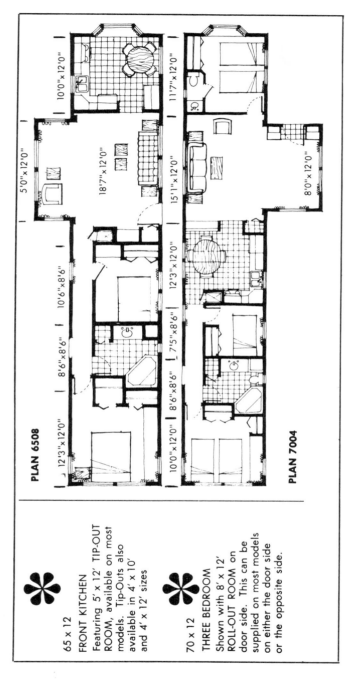

PLAN 6508

10'0"×12'0"

5'0"×12'0"

18'7"×12'0"

10'6"×8'6"

8'6"×8'6"

12'3"×12'0"

PLAN 7004

11'7"×12'0"

15'1"×12'0"

8'0"×12'0"

12'3"×12'0"

7'5"×8'6"

8'6"×8'6"

10'0"×12'0"

❁

65 x 12

FRONT KITCHEN

Featuring 5' x 12' TIP-OUT ROOM, available on most models. Tip-Outs also available in 4' x 10' and 4' x 12' sizes

❁

70 x 12

THREE BEDROOM

Shown with 8' x 12' ROLL-OUT ROOM on door side. This can be supplied on most models on either the door side or the opposite side.

Fig. 1-8. These drawings show what can be done with tipouts and expandos or roll-outs. The tipout (top) will give at most a five foot extension because it must be raised and lowered by muscle power. Roll-outs are considerably larger because they can be winched into place.

27

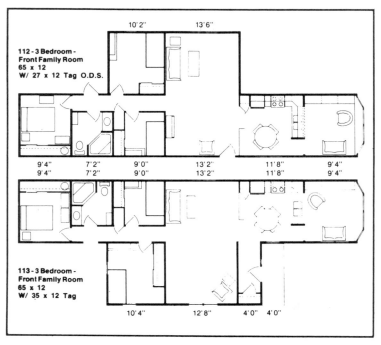

Fig. 1-9. The "tag-alongs," as seen in these drawings, can be used to even double the size of a mobile home because there is no limit to their width or length. The tag is virtually a home in itself with its own wheels and hitch.

She meant that it looked like the inside of a church. It had rough unpainted beams in the ceiling and a light hanging on big chains with bulbs that looked like candles. The walls were oak paneled. Doors, cupboards, and built-ins were massive oak. The furniture was all covered in blue velvet. There were bronze mugs and dishes on a sideboard. Light coming in through stained-glass windows gave the room a peaceful, church-like atmosphere. It was a man's room. I liked it. Wanda just sniffed and headed for the kitchen. It was a man's kitchen—solid and practical with heavy cutlery, bronze cookware, pewter, and dishes with English designs.

Wanda sniffed again. "No dishwasher," she said.

I despise automatic dishwashers because they're treacherous. I once reached into one for a spoon and it stabbed me in the wrist with a steak knife.

Wanda headed for the bathroom and opened a closet door. Again her nose wrinkled as she sniffed, "No washer-dryer."

It was a man's bathroom, practical and sensible. There was a built-in reading light at the toilet with a small book shelf and magazine rack. The shower had something else I've always wanted, a place to sit while you wash your feet. The shower and tub were molded in one piece with a built-in seat.

I remarked how I liked the tub and Cathy said, "You can get that tub in all our better homes, and it comes in various colors to match any decor."

Wanda sniffed and headed for the door. I sighed, and took a last look at the toilet book shelf and reading light.

Cathy pointed to another home. "That Park Estate has a dishwasher and an automatic washer-dryer in a full size utility room. It also has two expandos, or *pullouts* as Park Estate prefers to call them. The second expando is in the master bedroom, pushing it out to 19 feet in length. The living room is also 19 feet (Fig. 1-10)."

CLOSINGS AND THE SOFT SELL

"How long does it take to close a deal?" Wanda asked.

"On a conventional home, as you probably know, it can take over six months on VA or FHA, or even HUD mortgage loans. If you bought that Park Estate today by signing a sales agreement, *that* is the closing and you could move in tomorrow. In fact, it is actually possible to buy and move into a mobile home on the same day. That's why mobile homes are such a hit with young marrieds."

I could see Cathy watching us through long lashes. She said, "The base on this Park Estate is $9,000 without expandos. Loaded

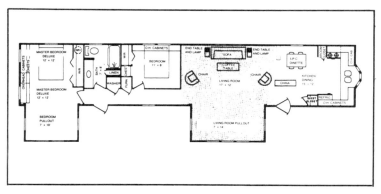

Fig. 1-10. This manufacturer calls expandos "pullouts" and makes them available in the living room and the master bedroom. Bedroom is now big enough for another double bed, or a sofa and two chairs.

Danville Public Library
Danville, Illinois

with everything, including two expandos, it will still be under $15,000. In some big cities, you can spend that much in one year renting an apartment with equivalent livability."

"Can we see it?" Wanda said.

"Certainly," Cathy said in her soft sell voice and manner.

Wheels were turning in my head as I thought of all the things I could do with the money we would save after we sold our home. It had been appraised at $39,900. We would be able to pay cash for a mobile home, and still have money left over.

I'm sure that Cathy knew exactly what was going on in my mind. This was all part of a Grand Plan by some very clever merchandisers. They had a great price, a great market and a tremendously attractive product—in many cases, *too* attractive. Cathy admitted this herself, which is why both Wanda and I could not help liking her. She was so honest. She wanted to sell us a mobile home, and she showed us many more, but she never hurried or grew impatient.

Coming out of the Park Estate, Cathy said, "Be patient, keep looking, we have something for everybody in unlimited variation, floor plans, and decorator themes like Contemporary, Modern, Provincial, Country English, Frontier, Early American, Oriental, and Spanish. Once you make your selection, you don't have to spend another cent for drapes, appliances, storm windows, or screens."

"How about modulars?" I asked.

"We have them. If you want something larger and more conventional in appearance than mobile homes, the modulars are the ultimate in flexibility, both in exterior design and interior decoration."

MODULARS

"Modulars do not come to the home site on their own wheels. They are a combination of modules or cubes which are shipped on flatbed trucks and set down by crane on a permanent foundation. You can start small and just keep adding on in almost any direction, winding up in time with a magnificent home costing half the price of a conventionally built home."

"Why is that?" Wanda asked.

"Modular units roll off assembly lines 365 days a year, with no delays for bad weather or because of a strike in some supplier industry. Everything that goes into homes is purchased in large quantities and is instantly available, no matter what your design requirements. Croydon has modulars available right now with basements and unfinished second floors (Fig. 1-11, 1-12).

"I am hoping you will buy from us," she said in that soft sell manner, "but whether you do or not, just remember there is more to buying a mobile home than signing the purchase agreement and a check. Your home must be set up on a proper foundation, it must be anchored down to withstand high winds, the plumbing must be

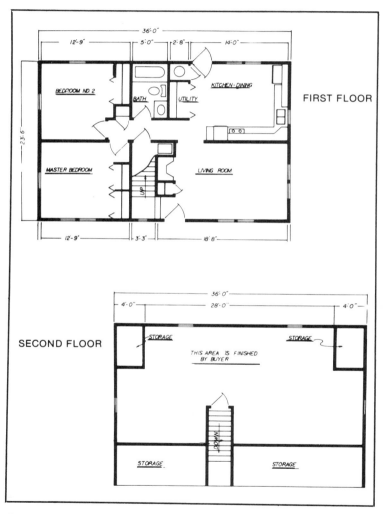

Fig. 1-11. This is Croyden's Cape Cod modular which has a second floor, to be finished off by the buyer.

protected from freezing. These things are all part of a package deal. You have nothing else to buy."

"How about air conditioning?" I interrupted.

HEATING AND COOLING

"It is not included as a standard item because in this area of cold winters, many buyers feel they are spending hundreds of extra dollars for something they will only use for a few hot days in the summer. It's awfully hard to convince them that even up in Minnesota, Canada, and Maine, air conditioning is almost as important as a good furnace."

"Why?" Wanda asked.

"Mobile homes, like automobiles, get awfully hot in the sun."

"Aren't they insulated?"

"Yes, and so are automobiles, but they still get hot. Everybody finds this out the hard way, then they put in window units, which look horrible and don't do the job. In the end, they always put in central air conditioning, and spend three times as much as it would have cost had it been done when the home was built."

"How much is air conditioning?"

"Between $450 and $650, depending on home size. But having it installed later can cost up to $1,500. My advice is, air conditioning is an absolute must."

"Anything else?"

Double Insulation

"Heating and cooling will be your two biggest utility expenses. I would recommend double insulation throughout the home. It doesn't cost much, yet it can save you hundreds of dollars. In areas of mild winters, I would recommend electric heat. In fact, I would prefer it even up here with our bad winters."

Electric Heat

"Why?" Wanda asked

"If you go away on a Florida vacation in the winter, you just set the thermostats down to about 50 degrees and you have no worries. With gas, you always have to worry about pilot lights blowing out on windy days, the furnace shutting itself off, and coming home to a mess of frozen pipes and toilets. You can have the same problem with an oil furnace. If the oil doesn't ignite in about 30 seconds, a safety device in the stack shuts the furnace off—and it *stays* off.

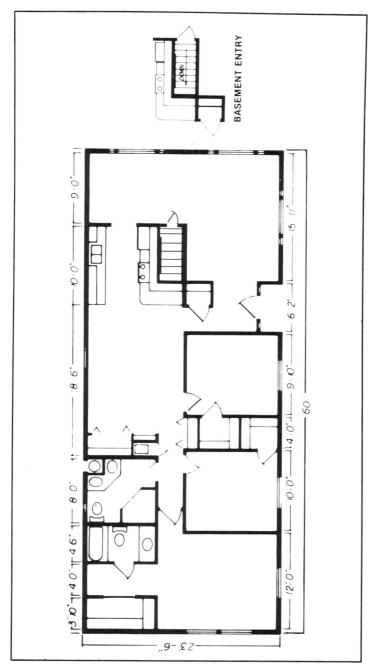

BASEMENT ENTRY

Fig. 1-12. This is a sixty foot ranch type modular home by Croyden which is set down by crane over a foundation and basement.

33

"With electric heat, you can be sure that even with temporary blackouts and power breakdowns, the electricity *always* comes back on, and so does your heat. Electricity is never off long enough for serious damage to occur. So, for people who are away from home often during the winter, I recommend electric heat because gas pilot lights are a definite problem in mobile homes."

"Why?"

"Short chimneys. It's only eight feet from the roof to the pilot light flame. Another option I recommend is the intercom system."

"Who needs *that*?" Wanda quickly interrupted.

Intercom System

"People like you," Cathy said.

"Why people like me?"

"For reasons of security. The intercom gives you a means of communication with anybody at the front door without opening it. You also can communicate with any room in the home, or pipe music to any room, collectively or individually."

"We'll buy it!" Wanda said quickly, bringing a smile to Cathy's lips.

WHY PEOPLE BUY MOBILE HOMES

It was this incident, along with the ever increasing tax load on property owners, that finally swayed our thinking that it was time to sell. When I mentioned this to Cathy, she said, "California has more super mobile home parks than any other state, except Florida. A California bank, which does a lot of mobile home financing, says that there is a great surge in that state by homeowners to unload their high tax homes and shift to apartments and mobile homes. Promoters are buying up all available land at a prodigious rate for development into mobile home communities."

A friend of mine on a local newspaper bought 19 acres on a corner plot 28 years ago for a future retirement home. Payments on the mortgage were $73 a month, taxes $16 a month. Today, although the mortgage is paid off, he pays $188 a month in taxes and was just assessed $60,000 for the sewer project. Interest will shoot this up to almost $100,000. Of course, the sheriff will take over his "retirement" home and sell it to some super developer.

After looking over a few more homes in the low price range. Cathy asked us what we thought of them. When we expressed amazement at how you could get so much for so little, she said, "Don't you believe it. You're not getting much and it's a poor way to save money. In the trade, those homes are referred to as 'Alabama Flash.'"

BEWARE OF ALABAMA FLASH

"What's that?"

"Alabama Flash is built by that 30 per cent of manufacturers who do not abide by the standard for mobile homes, ANSI A 119.1. This standard was developed by the highly respected American National Standards Institute in 1969 and covers all areas of mobile

Fig. 1-13. This emblem guarantees that the mobile home, whose serial number is registered, has been quality built in four basic areas: the body, frame, plumbing, and electrical system.

home construction. In those homes we just went through, did you notice all the unnecessary ornamentation and guady construction gimmicks, like those phony beams in the ceiling which simulated rough unfinished wood? They're just plastic and hollow inside. Homes like that catch the eye and make an impression because most people, yound ones especially, don't look too close on that first hurried trip through them. Later when they have bought and moved in, they begin to see behind the phony facade, the cheap plastic and tinsel. This type of construction originated in Alabama, which is how it got that name. So whenever anybody in the mobile home manufacturing industry puts something on or in their product to jazz up its appearance, it is derisively called 'Alabama Flash.' Fortunately over 70 per cent of American manufacturers abide by the standards."

"How can we tell which homes meet those standards?" Wanda asked.

ANSI STANDARDS FOR MOBILE HOMES

Cathy walked us across the street to a Croydon and pointed to a decal emblem on the siding next to the side entrance door. "Look for this emblem and serial number (Fig. 1-13). Only members of the Mobile Home Manufacturers Association who build homes to meet the specifications of ANSI Standards for Mobile Homes, A119.1., are permitted to use this decal. It is your guarantee that the home is quality built in four basic areas, the body, the frame, the plumbing, and the electrical system."

Standards for Body and Frame

"The body and frame of a mobile home are subjected to severe stresses and strains when traveling over even a smooth highway (Fig. 1-14). They are designed to withstand the stresses of road travel and high wind when properly anchored. Non-combustible pre-painted siding is used for strength and ease of maintenance. The wall framing is a network of interwoven 2 × 4 studs for maximum strength, durability and light weight for mobility if the home must be moved. With proper tie-down anchors, these walls have withstood winds up to hurricane force. The inside walls must meet ANSI standards both for durability and finish and the National Fire Protection Association's Standards for fire resistance with a flame-spread rating of Type 'C'.

"Roof trusses, on 16-inch centers, are of the girder design to provide great strength with minimum weight to bear heavy snow

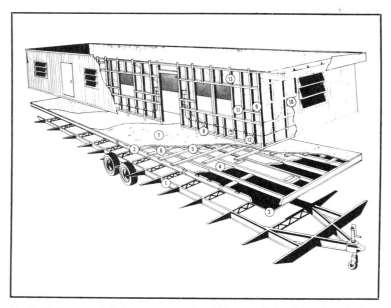

Fig. 1-14. Every mobile home owner should have a skeletal drawing similar to this supplied by the manufacturer, which will give him some idea where the wood framework is when he starts fastening things like awnings to the home. Fastening anything to the aluminum siding alone is a waste of time as the screws are easily pulled out.

loads (Fig. 1-15). The plumbing systems are all copper with water lines parallel to heat ducts to prevent freezing in winter. Water heaters are isolated from the home interior as a safety measure in case of gas leakage, and to prevent fumes from getting into the home. They are accessible through an outside door for easy servicing."

Standards for Heating Systems

"Standards for heating systems require that furnaces must be totally enclosed, and fresh air for combustion must come from the outside. This is an unusual safety feature not required for conventional home construction. On a wall of the furnace compartment, the manufacturer must post a certificate and a map of the United States to indicate the performance that can be expected from the heating system for the owner's section of the country , and also the snow load and wind velocity his roof will withstand. The standards also require a posting of the exact number and positions of each foundation support under the I-frame, with a recommendation that only solid cement footing blocks be used, not hollow building blocks which can break and collapse."

You Get What You Pay For

I was both impressed and disturbed. "Then all the bad publicity mobile homes have been getting is true—junky homes *are* being sold, at least 30 per cent, you said."

"I didn't say that. I said that 30 per cent of American manufacturers did not subscribe to the ANSI Sandards. That doesn't mean they all turn out Alabama Flash. Sure, they turn out low cost homes in the average price range of $4,500 to $12,000. But what do you expect to get for $4,500? You can't even buy a Volkswagen bus for that kind of money. As I said before, the only guide you need to a good home is the price tag. If you want a Cadillac, then be prepared to pay a Cadillac price. If you are considering the purchase of a mobile home to save money, stay away from the low price tags. They may be cheaper to buy and finance initially, but in the long run they are more expensive. Our three most costly homes here are actually the *cheapest*. Over the long pull, you will spend less for repairs and changes. You will lose less in depreciation, and if you ever sell, you will get a higher price. If you ever move, they won't fall apart on some county road and wipe you out in one big bang, if, to save money, you hire some local transport outfit to move you, and they don't have insurance."

Cathy's sales manner proves the truth of a hairy old bromide: "Honesty is the best policy." I had come only to look, but now I wanted to buy, and that frightened me. So I stalled with, "Can we have some literature?" This is an old escape route if you want to get away before you start signing things. Cathy said, "Let's go to the office."

The "office" was just another mobile home. It was a yellow and cream Croydon with a "tag" that was almost as big as the main home. It had a real porch with large concrete steps and black iron railings. There was an intercom speaker to the left of two very attractive doors with a button for "talk" and "listen."

We stepped into a foyer with a flagstone floor and glass skylight overhead. We could see through black Moorish-like grillwork into the living room. And what a room! It looked like the board room of the Chase Manhattan Bank with wood paneled walls and thick rug.

I think it is a matter of contrasts. Mobile homes are unimposing on the outside, and you are unprepared for what you see suddenly on the inside. It's quite an experience.

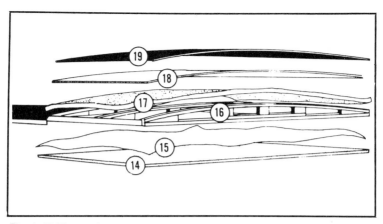

Fig. 1-15. The roof trusses, 16 above, are 16 inches apart and their outline can be easily seen on the roof. It is important when working on the roof, fixing leaks or coating with roof paint, to walk and stand on the trusses because between them is just thin galvanized steel. The more you buckle this metal, the more water it will hold, the more it will leak, and the more mosquitos it will hatch.

Wanda's eyes were gaping again and she asked weakly, "How much does *this* cost?"

"*Don't tell her!*" I said quickly, holding a hand up in mock horror. "I'm still recovering from open heart surgery."

There was forced laughter all around the room. Suddenly I realized there were six or seven other people in that huge room. Yet they were lost in the vastness of that wood-paneled cathedral!

Cathy introduced us all around. They were all sales people, two of them girls in hotpants and striped T-shirts. I wondered why they weren't outside selling or giving away donuts. A balding fat man was sitting behind a big conference desk, toying with a long movie-producer cigar. Beside him in a black leather chair an older woman was sitting cross-legged like a hooker in the lobby of the Holiday Inn. Her eyes were shadowed green, her lips were platinum. She wore red pantyhose, a mini-mini skirt, and white sandals with Roman style ribbons wrapped around her calves. When she got up out of that chair, she winced like her arthritis was killing her.

"Did you want some literature, honey?" she purred.

I was beginning to feel a little nervous when Fat Man held a hand over the desk. "I'm B.J. Goldfine. I'm the owner."

If he had said: "I'm Akim Tamiroff," I wouldn't have been surprised. He even had the same accent as that old veteran movie actor. He waved that big cigar around the room like a field marshall's baton.

"You like this?" he asked grandly.

I sighed deeply, then for some strange reason I did something foolish. I said: "This trailer is way out of my financial reach."

They're Not Trailers

It got very cold in that big room and I could feel hostility in the air. Remember this when you go looking at mobile homes. Don't *ever* call mobile homes "trailers." That's a dirty word. You could get pneumonia from the sudden chill.

The arthritic sex kitten came to my rescue. She handed me the literature with a gentle smile. "I'm Mrs. Goldfine. Are you sure you want that literature, honey? We don't sell trailers here."

I swallowed hard. "Sorry, I meant to say mobile home."

"Do you know the difference?"

"I think so . . . "

"I don't think you do." She turned to Cathy, "Honey, this is your deal. Explain to him the difference between a mobile home and a trailer."

Cathy looked embarrassed, almost like she was ashamed of me. She said gently, as if talking to a child, "A trailer is something you hitch up to the back of your car and pull up to Devil's Lake for a weekend of fishing. Mobile homes are fitted with wheels, yes, but only so they can be rolled from the factory to a permanent lot. After that the wheels are removed and the hitch sometimes is cut off with a torch, then all kinds of things are added on and attached, which finally make it as permanent as a brick church."

"Yeah, yeah, I know. It's just that I was so overwhelmed by the size and opulence of this beautiful . . . "

"You forgot to cover up your prejudices, honey."

"I'm not prejudiced, Mrs. Goldfine."

"Then why did you call this a trailer?"

"Everybody calls mobile homes trailers."

"Not everybody, honey. I don't think you *like* mobile homes."

"That isn't true, Mrs. Goldfine. I like *this*."

"Then why do you say it is out of your reach?"

"I don't know. How much *is* this?"

"Give a guess."

"Fifty thousand."

"You're half right, honey. This home has the livability of 50 thousand, but only costs 24 thousand—and completely furnished as you see it, excluding, of course, the office equipment. There are no hidden extras, there is nothing else to buy. You just move in your clothes and toothbrushes. It's that easy."

CLOSING COSTS

"Easy!" I almost shouted. "You must be kidding! The last time we bought a home, it took six months. At the closing, there were ten people sitting around a big table at the Louisville Title Company. I was signing papers and checks for a half hour. A friend of mine just paid out $1,400 in settlement costs when he bought a 20 year old home for $28,000. He's still in shock."

"I know," Mrs. Goldfine said, going through some papers on her husband's desk. "I save this copy of the Sunday paper because there was a story in the home section about closing costs. It listed all the things you had to pay. Here they are:

"The costs connected with getting a mortgage.

"The costs of protecting you and the property you are buying.

"The costs of anything you are buying from the seller that wasn't included in the price of the house.

"Credit reports.

"Appraisal fee.

"Survey.

"Title insurance.

"Service charge of 1½ percent for arranging the loan, not to be confused with points.

"Mortgage interest from closing to date of first payment. Can sometimes be over $100.

"First payment on the mortgage, paid in advance at the closing. Can be over $200.

"Fire insurance, first year premium paid in advance.

"Schedule of mortgage payments, just a few dollars.

"Prorations. If there is half a tank of heating oil, the buyer must pay for it.

"The seller must pay assessments and his part of the next tax bill.

"Payment to seller for things you agreed to buy from him, like garden tools, furniture, etc.

"Escrow fee.

"Legal fees.

"Recording fees of the deed and mortgage.

"The matter of points, which the seller always pays to compensate banks for making FHA and VA loans at less then the going rate of interest on conventional home loans. This can be $500 and up.

"All these things can add up to a bundle."

"Now here's the good news," Mr. Goldfine said, waving that big cigar again. "There are no closing costs when you buy a mobile home. No vultures waiting around to pick your bones. On a cash sale, a mobile home deal can be closed in less then five minutes, the time it takes to sign your name a few times. Financed deals take an average of two days, sometimes with good credit the same day."

"Why is it so easy?" Wanda asked. "Why no closing costs?"

"No real estate is involved, honey."

"Isn't a home real estate?"

"Only if land is included. Buying a mobile home is like buying an automobile."

MOBILE HOME TITLES

"Isn't there a title involved? I asked. "A title search alone sometimes takes weeks."

"There's no title searching on a mobile home. That means no big abstracts to type, no lawyers to read the abstracts. In Ohio you get the same kind of a title you get when you buy a car. That's all."

"Amazing," I said.

"Do you people now own a home?" Cathy asked.

Suddenly I was embarrassed. "I suppose we should have waited until our home was sold before coming here."

"Not at all, honey. We go through this all the time. Most of the homes we sell are to people just like you who already own a home."

"We've got about forty deals on the back burner right now," her husband added. "They're just waiting for VA or FHA loan approvals."

"Suppose there isn't any closing," I said. "What happens then?"

"Nothing."

"Just nothing?"

"What do you mean, honey?"

"Suppose I get an offer on my home, I accept, then the deal falls through because my buyer can't get a mortgage loan. That means no closing. And suppose I had signed up to buy a mobile home here and made a down payment."

"We would refund your money," Mrs. Goldfine said, "unless you wanted to try again to sell your home."

"I don't believe it," Wanda said.

"What don't you believe, honey?"

"That refund part."

"What do you mean?"

"She means refunding down payment money is un-American," I said.

Mrs. Goldfine screamed with laughter, then hacked and coughed until her eyes watered. This made mascara run down her cheeks. "It's all spelled out in the agreement, honey."

"What is?"

"The contingency closing clause. That's your escape hatch in case something blows the deal on your home. On the purchase agreement, we type: 'final sale contingent on closing of such-and-such property.' If we didn't put that clause in there, nobody would ever sign a purchase agreement until they sold their homes."

"Does everybody do that?" I asked.

"I can't speak for everybody, honey. I just know *we* do. And we sell more homes then anybody else in the business because people will sign a contract if you give them an escape hatch."

"I can't believe it," Wanda said.

"Is there something you don't understand?" Cathy asked.

"Yes and no."

"You haven't seen the rest of this Croydon. Why don't you go through it by yourselves. Take your time. If you think of some more questions, just yell."

We did as she suggested. The Croydon was incredibly large. It had three bedrooms, two full baths, a big family room, and a separate laundry room with a washer and dryer. It was lush and fabulous and we were scared to death. Like so many people, we had come with pre-conceived notions about "house trailers." People come to "just look," to smugly confirm their prejudices. Then, they get hit in their psyches by one of the shrewdest merchandising campaigns ever devised. And before they know what hit them, they have bought a mobile home.

It is so easy to buy a mobile home that it is difficult for middle and older people to avoid over-buying. They usually have more than enough money, after selling their homes, so the tendency is to splurge. (The young marrieds, with no equity in real estate, don't have this problem.)

And this was our problem. I knew we would have the money, after selling our home, and I knew Wanda was enthralled by those kitchens and all that luxury. So, while we were still limp and unable to resist, Cathy steered us into a small room next to the bathroom.

Fig. 1-16. The author's darkroom, which was custom built at the factory. This room would normally be supplied with a window. The ceiling light is also an exhaust fan with two pullchains, one for white light, one for safelight. The room is air-conditioned. Custom changes of this type can be performed by the manufacturer at the time of construction, usually at substantial savings to the customer when compared to his cost to do the same work.

She said, "This is my office. Normally, this room is a guest bedroom with a double bed. Now, what do you think?"

I looked around the room and up at the bedroom window. "Can I order some changes?"

"Like what?"

"That window. I don't want it."

Her blue eyes widened. "Why?"

"Windows are a nuisance in a photographic darkroom. You're constantly fighting with them to keep out little pinholes of light. It would be so much simpler if that window was just eliminated when my home is built—and maybe lot cheaper."

"If you want to convert this into a darkroom, you won't want any furniture or beds in here, will you?"

"Nothing, just a big sink and plenty of cupboards. Will they do it?

"I don't see why not. Last month we had a man who wanted to convert the utility room into a chemistry lab. The washer-dryer had to be changed to a stacked combination and moved to a closet in the big bathroom."

CUSTOM CHANGES

"The manufacturer refers to this as custom changes. They're very cooperative, so long as it isn't too far out. They put in two stainless sinks for this man, and a long workbench with plenty of drawers and cupboards. He was very happy with the results."

"How much did it cost?"

"About $200."

"That's all?" I gasped. "Gosh, I was planning on spending about a grand to fix up this room."

"That's ridiculous! If you can get by with stainless steel kitchen sinks—say, does a darkroom sink have to be all in one piece?"

"No, why?"

"The factory won't have a special sink made for you, but if you can get by with what they already have, they'll put in all the sinks you need. You can save a bundle if you let them custom build you a darkroom. It won't cost anything to eliminate a window. In fact, they'll give you a credit for the window framing, the bed and furniture. This credit will pay for the extra sinks, cupboards, drawers, and workbenches."

Cathy was right. We saved at least $2,000 by having the factory custom build my darkroom (Fig. 1-16), my den office, and Wanda's hobby sewing room in the back bedroom. The large family room became my office, with a built-in desk along one wall and six drawers. Ceiling-high bookshelves covered the other walls. They did the same thing in what normally would have been the master bedroom in back, which is Wanda's "workshop." The credit for furniture in these rooms reduced the conversion cost down to a little over $400. I couldn't have done it myself for less than $3,000.

As Cathy said, "This is one time when you can't save money doing it yourself. Let *them* do it and save a bundle."

2

Save in the
Right Park

It's so easy to buy a mobile home. It's so hard to believe it when you do.

The first thing I said the next morning when I sat down at the breakfast table was, "Wow, what a crazy nightmare I had. I dreamed we bought a mobile home."

When Wanda poured my coffee, she put a slip of paper on the table beside my cup. It was a yellow copy of the purchase agreement for one Croydon mobile home, total price with air conditioning, custom modifications, and sales tax: $26,985.

"Why didn't you stop me?" I groaned, holding my head.

"We don't have to go through with the deal until we sell our house. It says so right there in the contingency clause. So stop your moaning."

I felt a little better after that, but not for long because I could sense that Wanda was disappointed when I made no effort to list our home with some realty company. She never said anything, just moped around. Then things started to happen.

A small news item in the business section of the local newspaper caught my eye. It was about a real estate salesman selling his fine suburban home in exclusive Ottawa Hills and buying a mobile home. I thought, gosh, if a top salesman like Dave Garrison, with annual sales of over a million, is giving up on conventional housing, maybe he knows something.

When I phoned, he hung up on me. I guessed maybe he was just sick and tired of answering the phone and people calling wanting to know why.

I tried another approach. I wrote to him, care of his business address, and asked him to come out and list my home. He did. After I signed the 90-day contract, he asked if I planned to buy another home. I said I did. When he asked if he could show me some of his listings, I then told him I was planning on buying a mobile home. When he asked why, I hit him with "Why did you?"

He replied, "To protect my equity. I had to get out while there was still time. My home was on a corner acre of land in what was once wooded rural country with no improvements. The few of us who lived there had septic tanks, and artesian wells and used LP gas for heat. Now, the city is growing fast in that direction. City improvements are in the visible future. That means paved streets, paved sidewalks and curbs, sanitary sewers, and storm sewers. With corner property, you get assessed twice by the footage on each street.

"The assessments for all those improvements would have wiped out my entire equity and been a financial load I could not carry. I would have been unable to sell the property, and unable to make the payments on both my mortgage and assessments. So I sold the property before this fact became generally known. I got a good price and my equity is now safely invested and earning money."

"Did you use any of the equity to buy your mobile home?" I asked.

"Only enough for the down payment."

"How come?"

DON'T PAY CASH

"A banker once told me, 'Never use your own money to buy something that depreciates in value.' That is the key to success in a capitalistic world. If I were going to invest money in the mobile home industry, it would be in the parks, not the homes."

"Talking about parks," I said quickly, "where do you plan on putting your new mobile home?"

"I'm still undecided."

"Why?"

"I found out after much study that there is a great deal more to mobile home parks than a piece of land, available water, sewage and utility connections. Buying a mobile home is easy. If you look at only the best, your choice is narrowed down to just a few. But where to put that home is a problem."

"Why?"

THE CHEAP LOTS

"Most people who buy a mobile home are concerned only with saving money, so they go where the lot rentals are the cheapest. In the end, this turns out to be the most *expensive* way to go because they are unhappy. This forces them to either sell their home at a loss, or move it at considerable expense. Incidently, I don't know if anybody ever told you, but mobile homes are *not* mobile as the word implies. You don't just back up a tractor and haul away. A friend of mine moved his home just three miles to another park and it cost him around $3,500. He told me it would have been easier to move one of the pyramids of Giza. That is why selection of the right park is so important. It's so expensive to move—and to be evicted. You also must think about that. If you're not compatible with the park's many rules and regulations, you could get yourself involved in endless hassles with park management, finally getting yourself evicted.

"This is what happened just recently to a widow up in Monroe who was evicted for buying two goldfish. That's right, two tropical goldfish. Her park had a rule against bringing in exotic pets without permission. Of course, this rule was obviously intended to keep out weird pets like boa constrictors, alligators, and monkeys. However, the rule did not exclude tropical goldfish, so it became a convenient device to get rid of her."

RULES AND REGULATIONS

"The widow's troubles started when she fought against the park's many rules and regulations, like the one which forbade the drying of clothes outside. She's an oldtimer who believes that clothes must be aired and purified in the sun. Then she kept parking her car on the street, which is another rule violation. Finally, just to get even with the park manager who she hated, she stopped paying her rent as a protest against being "persecuted," as she said. That was her big mistake. She could have been evicted for this alone, but out of consideration for her credit rating, the park evicted her on the exotic pet rule.

"This is something to consider because many men will find themselves incompatible with those rules and regulations, especially when they can't do any repair or tune-up work on their cars. This is a fairly common rule in all three, four and five star parks."

THE STAR RATING SYSTEM

"Who decides how many stars a park gets?" I asked.

"The Woodall Publishing Company, in their annual *Mobile*

Home & Park Directory. They have professional inspectors all over the country who visit the parks once a year and check them out, after which they are rated from one to five stars. There are over 13,000 parks in this country and they're all rated."

"Where do you get that book?"

"Any book store, or you can order it direct. They're in Highland Park, Illinois."

"What's a five star park like?"

He removed a thick paperback book from his attache case, and thumbed through it.

A Five Star Park Description

"It says: 'Five star parks are the finest. They should be nearly impossible to improve. Their quality must be diligently maintained. They must be well planned and laid out with a spacious appearance. They must be in a good location in regards to accessibility and desirable neighborhood. In some areas, parks should be enclosed by high hedges or ornamental fencing. They should have wide paved streets in perfect condition, curbs or lawns edged to streets, sidewalks from street to home. They must have street lights and street signs. Homes must be set back from the street. The park must have an exceptionally attractive entrance and sign. All homes must have patios of at least 320 sq. ft, excepting double wides. There must be paved two-car off street parking with carports, or a planned parking area. All homes must be skirted with metal skirting, or ornamental wood or stone. There must be awnings, cabanas or porches on all homes. All hitches must be removed, or concealed, all tanks concealed. There must be recreation available with some or all of the following, swimming, shuffleboard, horseshoe pitching, golf course, hobby shop, hobby classes, games, potlucks, dances or natural recreational facilities. The park must have a beautifully equipped recreation hall with kitchen, room for community gatherings, tiled restrooms. There must be uniform storage sheds, or central storage facilities. All homes in park must be late models and in excellent condition. There must be a 60 per cent occupancy in the park to judge quality of residents and park's ability to maintain a five star rating between inspections. All empty lots must be grassed, gravelled or otherwise well maintained. If pets or children are allowed, there must be a place for them to play and run without cluttering the streets and yards. The majority of five star parks are for adults only. There must be superior management interested in comfort of residents and maintenance of the park.'"

"Are there any five star parks around here?"

"None, not even in the whole state. The best we have in Ohio is a four star called The Willows in Akron. It's an adult park with no pets allowed."

Where the Best Parks Are

"What's the best we have around here?"

"A three plus."

"What's that 'plus' mean?"

"Better then three star, but not quite good enough to be four. And you won't do any better in Michigan, Indiana, Illinois, or even New York State. Arizona only has one five star, but they've got 10 four-plus, which is so close to a five star that you can't tell them apart unless you're a professional inspector."

I groaned. "Not even one five star in the whole state. I can't believe it."

"I can't either. I've seen those five stars in Florida and they're absolutely fabulous. Florida has 108 five stars and 41 four-plus. California has 105 five stars but they also have 124 four-plus parks. California and Florida are mobile home paradise."

"Why nothing in the rest of the country?" I asked.

"I really don't know. Most five stars are strictly for adults and I was told that you can't maintain a top quality rating if you allow children and pets."

"Why?"

"With children you have juvenile crime, like theft, break-ins when people are away, and vandalism. Nothing tears a park down quicker then that."

"Maybe I shouldn't ask, but what's a one star park got, if anything?"

The One Star Parks

"Only the basic essentials, like water, sewage, electricity and telephone. For heat you will usually have LP gas or oil in an outside tank in back. The streets are dirt or crushed stone. There are no lawns, just whatever grows. The homes are close together and come in all sizes, many with wheels and hitches still attached and visible. These parks are only a slight improvement over a trailer court."

"Ugh!" I said. "And the best we have around here is a three-plus?"

"Don't knock it now. There's actually very little difference in the outward appearance between a three-plus and a five star, until you look real close. For example, in a five star you will never see a $6,000 single wide right next door to a $24,000 double wide. The homes will be quite uniform in quality with a minimum standard of $15,000. The five stars will have more recreational facilities, a resident park manager available at all times, and security protection. Sometimes the only reason a park will drop to a three-plus rating is because the manager doesn't live in the park, and isn't available around the clock and on weekends. Also, five stars with a resident manager are more rigid in their enforcement of the rules and regulations."

"What's the rating on Blossom Heath Estates?"

"The best for this area, a three-plus."

How To Avoid Being Fenced In

"Now, if you don't like being fenced in by endless rules and regulations, you might be happier in a lower rated park, like a two or one star where you can putter on your car and not be harassed by the manager. But, if you are an orderly person, then you will certainly want to live in an orderly community with rules and regulations that are enforced. However, therein lies a problem. I have discovered that all three-plus parks are not necessarily equal. They may look pretty much the same, but it's not the same when you live there."

"Why?"

"Some of these parks do not enforce their rules and regulations. That makes for a disorderly community and a bad place to put your investment. So, in spite of their high ratings, these are bad parks for an orderly person who is trying to save money."

HOW TO RECOGNIZE A "BAD" PARK

"How can you tell a bad park?" I asked.

"By driving through it. Count the FOR SALE signs in windows. Watch for TV antennas on roofs. All three-plus parks have a central antenna system and forbid private antennas because they are supposed to be an 'esthetic abomination' the owners say. If you see antennas on roofs, it means one of two things; either the central antenna isn't any good, or the park is lax in enforcing their own rules.

"If you see cars parked with one wheel on the sidewalk (Fig. 2-1), that is another tell-tale sign of a poorly managed park. Watch for junk cars (Fig. 2-2), which would *never* be tolerated in a good park. Stop and talk to one of the residents, and ask if police or

Fig. 2-1. Cars parked like this with one wheel on the sidewalk are a good indication of poor management and a bad park. If you move here, you will not be saving money because when you get disgusted enough, you will move, and that costs money.

sheriff's patrol cars answer many calls in the park. This is a sure sign of a bad park because if police must come to the park to settle internal problems, it means there is no manager available on the premises, so tenants have no recourse but to call the police (Fig. 2-3) for help. Park residents would never call the police if a manager was available because the police never settle anything. They just come there, usually an hour after being called, write down a few things on their clipboards, and leave.

"The last thing to watch for, and perhaps the most important, is children of all ages (Fig. 2-4). They are the biggest problem in all mobile home communities, and the reason why most five stars are restricted to adults only. Sometimes there are cases of vandalism and harassment. Without good management, the finest looking three-plus park can quickly become an aluminum jungle with residents hiding behind double-bolted doors, the police telephone number close at hand."

The So-Called "Adult Section"

"When I went to one of the three-plus parks to check, the manager told me, 'We have a section reserved exclusively for adults.'

Fig. 2-2. Junk cars and other such hideous eyesores would never be tolerated in any well managed park. Regardless of the star rating, if you see anything like this when driving through a park, just keep on going.

"That sounds good, but it doesn't mean a thing, I was told. So I asked, 'How do you keep the young people out of the adult section? How do you keep them from prowling around late at night committing acts of vandalism?'

Fig. 2-3. Beware of any park where the police make frequent calls because it happens only where there is bad management, and this can mean expensive trouble for you. Find out about problems like this by talking to tenants of the park.

Fig. 2-4. Nothing can ruin a good park faster than children of all ages if they are not controlled by both parents and management. The little ones will play in the streets and the big ones will prowl around at night destroying property. This could be your biggest and most expensive problem.

"The manager looked confused for a moment, then he recovered, and said, 'This is private property. We have rules and regulations covering just about everthing that might interfere with a tenant's right to be secure and happy in his home.'

"How about motorcycles and hot rods without mufflers racing through the park?" I asked.

"He said, 'We are working now on a plan to have two security guards, one in a marked jeep. We plan on completely enclosing this park with an 8-foot barbwire fence (Fig. 2-5). The second guard will be stationed at the entrance to keep out motorcycles, hot rods and troublemakers.'

"I said, 'How do you control vandalism by young people who live in the park?'"

Kiss of Death: The 30-Day Eviction Notice

"He said, 'We have a powerful weapon of persuasion, called the 30-day eviction notice. In mobile home communities, nothing frightens a homeowner more than a threat of eviction. It is called the Kiss of Death. When you read one of our leases, you will understand why.'

"I read one of those leases and, believe me, it is a frightening document. When I showed it to my lawyer, he just shook his head. He couldn't believe it. I have a copy here in my case. Let me read you two paragraphs.

"Item 11. *'Tenant shall comply with all laws, ordinances, and regulations of applicable government authorities, and will comply with rules and regulations of the park, which herein become a part of this agreement.'*

"Item 17. *'If default be made by Tenant in any of the covenants or agreements contained herein, Landlord may, at any time during which such default shall exist, without notice declare this agreement to be ended and re-enter the Tenant's premises, or part thereof, either with or without process of law, and remove any and all persons and any property from the Landlord's premises using such force as may be reasonably necessary so to do, but without any prejudice to any remedies which Landlord may have at law or in equity, and Tenant*

Fig. 2-5. In some areas a park that is not protected by a good fence is in trouble, as this one was before the fence was installed. A great deal of trouble and crime come into the park from the outside, and not necessarily through the main entrance gate. Motorcycle gangs like to race through fields and woods and come into a park the back way, between homes. This fence could save you the expense of moving.

hereby expressly waives all rights to any notices or demands under any law of the State of Ohio, whether relating to forcible entry and detainer or otherwise.'

"What this all means is that if, in addition to the park's rules and regulations, you break any ordinance or governmental law, even the most minor misdemeanor, this lease can be declared in default. Acts of vandalism, even by a minor, are violations of law. So is removing the muffler from an automobile or motorcycle, so is speeding through the park, so is parking on sidewalks. So is trespassing on another tenant's lot, so is removing property, so is excessive noise, so is burning garbage and polluting the air—the list is endless. As you can see, park management has a double-barreled shotgun, the public law and their own rules and regulations aimed at your head. As the park manager said: 'It is a powerful weapon.' "

Juvenile Crime

"With all these powerful weapons, why is there so much juvenile crime in mobile home parks? Why are so many park tenants forming associations to protect their interests, and give them leverage in dealing with management and state legislatures? The president of one of these park groups told me 'It's all a matter of economics. None of the parks around here are filled. Two new ones, representing multi-million dollar investments, are less than a third filled. To get a national rating, a park must have at least a 60 per cent occupancy at all times. So owners are reluctant to evict anybody. When they do enforce their own rules to evict, it is to serve their own vested interests. For example, non-payment of rent doesn't hurt me, it only hurts them. So they evict. But things that hurt only me they ignore.' As long as it doesn't affect the park's image or cost them money, you can get by with almost anything, as happened in one park recently, I was told.

"A little girl, who had been waiting for a schoolbus came rushing back home, and breathlessly told her mother, 'Some boy and girl are wrestling in back of Mr. Snyder's truck. They haven't any clothes on.'

"When the mother called the sheriff's substation, she was told, 'That park is private property. We can't go in there for that. Now if you see them again on Airport Highway, you call us back.'

"The mother reported this later to the park manager, and he said, 'What a man does in his own car parked in his own driveway is none of your business. If it bothers you, don't look.' "

"What is the name of that park?" I asked.

He told me. "And if you're wondering how it's rated nationally, it isn't because it's a new park and only about a third filled. The backers are frantic, I hear, because they borrowed heavily. You can be sure they aren't leaning on anybody who pays his rent. They're so desperate, they recently sold a home and rented a lot to a couple with 11 kids—and the single wide they bought only has three bedrooms."

"Good grief!" I gasped.

"That family reminds me of another problem children bring into a mobile community, and everybody sweeps under the rug—taxes and school overcrowding. When I asked the park manager in Woodville if the schools in the area could handle all the kids from his park, he said cautiously, 'They're not overcrowded *yet*.' "

Taxes and School Overcrowding

"I said, 'You're only half filled.'

"He interrupted with, 'If there is danger of overcrowding the schools, we have promised township authorities we will stop accepting tenants with children.'

'How about new children born in the park?'

"He was annoyed by that question. 'Why do you ask?'

" 'As a prospective tenant of your park, I was thinking of future tax problems. If park baby births eventually overcrowd the township schools, there will be new school levies and increases in real estate taxes, which you will pass on to the tenants in rent increases.'

" 'We are considering a limit on children per home.'

" 'How many?'

" 'Two per home.'

" 'What happens when a two child mother gets pregnant?'

The Two Child Park

" 'We will gently suggest to the couple that they make arrangements to move elsewhere. We won't push or set down a rigid time schedule, but we will insist they move. Nobody has asked such a question before. Why do you?'

" 'To save money,' I said quickly. 'Putting my new mobile home into the wrong park could be a very expensive mistake for me.'

" 'You're right about taxes,' he said. 'There definitely will be levies for schools, there will be salary increases for teachers, there will be water rate increases, another for sewage. And since we own the land, the cost will pass on directly to us and we, in turn, will pass it on to our tenants in rent increases. But remember one thing, these costs are spread out over 465 lots. A mere dollar increase in the rent brings us over $5,000 a year to help pay those increases. So, as you can see, tax increases in a mobile home community are almost painless because, unlike the poor individual homeowner, you don't carry the burden alone.' "

Lot Rentals

" 'What are your lot rentals?' I asked.

" 'The regular lots, which average about 45 × 85 feet, are $60 a month. The corner lots, many considerably larger, are $70 a month.'

" 'Isn't that rather high?' I said.

" 'Not for a three-plus park.'

" 'But you aren't rated yet.'

" 'That doesn't really matter because we have all the necessary qualifications. Of course, you can rent a lot for $25 and set up your fine mobile home in a junky trailer park with dirt roads and oil drums set up on 2× 4 stands. At night you can hear your neighbor just five feet away snoring. If that doesn't bother you, the two hunting dogs living under his trailer will blow your mind some night when they start baying at the moon or barking at flies. If you think that is the way to save money, lots of luck.'

"He was right," Garrison said. "Most of the people who set up their homes in low rent parks just to save money eventually become so disgusted, they just walk out one day and let the banks take over. In a recent newspaper column by Sylvia Porter, she said repossession of mobile homes was reaching alarming proportions, something like 20,000 a month. There is an old Chinese proverb, 'Nobody ever runs away from happiness.' People who are happy in their homes and their parks will never run out no matter what the state of their finances. They have to live *somewhere*, so they come up with the money because they know that a mobile home, like an automobile, can be quickly repossessed with just one missed payment."

"What did you think of the park managers you talked with?" I asked.

"That last one over in Woodville was the least abrasive, the least annoyed with my questioning. The others were a bunch of meatheads, except for the one over at Blossom Heath Estates who just looked confused and unhappy.

"I think all park managers are unhappy. It must be the nature of the surly brutes. They are a much unloved bunch. That one over in Holland drives 40 miles to work every day from another town. This is another thing that can lower a park's national rating a half star because if the manager does not live in, he must at least be readily available by telephone. This one has an unlisted number. You know, it's amazing how these owners will invest two million to develop a fine park which *could* get a five star rating, then they hire some castoff misfit to manage it, like that one over in Perrsburg everybody calls 'Jaws.' I would have liked to live there, except for him."

"Why?" I asked. "If it's just another three-plus park, what difference does it make?"

"More than you think. All three-plus parks are equal in the ratings, but some are more equal than others."

THE RATINGS CAN MISLEAD

"Those ratings can be very misleading. For example, all three-plus parks have sanitary sewers, but not the same kind. And therein lies a problem. Parks within the corporate limits will tie into the municipal sewage system. Parks out in the county have their own sewage disposal plants. Most of them are inadequate for the job."

Odors From Sewage Plants

"All the parks supply so called 'free' water, but not the same amount. On the one hand they will require you to diligently water your lawn during dry hot weather. Then they will warn you against using too much water, or even threaten to install a meter and make you pay for the excess, whatever that means."

The "Free" Water Problem

"There is a residue which has to be scraped off the top in the holding tanks about once a week. This should be hauled away or buried. In this plant, it was just spread out on the ground to dry. As it often is with these things, nobody took into consideration the prevailing west-southwest winds when they located the sewage plant and dry-out beds on the southwest corner of the park. So eight months out of every year, there is an odor problem."

The Garbage Problem

"All parks supply a garbage pick-up service once a week, but not the same amount. Some have unlimited pick-up, some have a limit of six bags, some only two bags or cans. Some let you worry about those endless cartons and boxes that come with almost everything you buy these days. At Christmas, when everything you buy for the kids comes disassembled in a box, cardboard trash can be a monumental problem. When you drive through a park on your inspection tour, if you see one of those huge carton containers that once housed a refrigerator being used as a playhouse by children on an empty lot, you will know why."

Grass Clippings and Leaves

"If the park limits you on garbage pick-up, what do you do with the grass clippings and leaves in the fall? An average lawn cutting once a week will fill two plastic bags. In the spring, raking of dead grass will often fill 10 bags. The same with leaves in the fall. You will not be saving money in some parks if you have to pay to have these things hauled away."

Where Does All The Water Go?

"All three-plus parks have paved streets, curbs, and sidewalks, but they don't all have storm sewers. Where does all the water go when it rains for a week? Will it wind up around and under your home? Will you drive through six inches of water in the streets? Will it just lay in the empty lots and breed mosquitoes?

Is The Central Antenna Any Good?

"All parks have community or central antennas, but they're not all the same. Some are good, some are lousy. Some bring in only the local channels, but you can get them on you rabbit ears, so why pay for a hook-up into the central antenna? Some parks have Cablevision. If TV is important to you, this is something that should be checked out thoroughly because once you move into a park, you are stuck with something you can never change. If you put up your own antenna, they'll harass you and threaten you until you take it down. You'll just be wasting money—just like you wasted money when you moved into that park in the first place."

Is The Recreation Any Good?

"All three-plus parks have recreational facilities like a swimming pool, community building, and swings for the kids, but they're not all the same. The park in Holland has 465 lots, but the swimming pool is no bigger than the one I had in my own back yard. With all those people using it, the water gets pretty polluted. In fact, last summer the county board of health ordered the pool closed for that very reason. Only one park around here has a tennis court. The community buildings vary from ridiculous to lavish. The park over in Perrysburg spent so much money on a community building, swimming pool and tennis court, they had nothing left for the park itself, which is why all the homes sit directly on the ground with no anchoring. That's the reason they were rated only two-plus stars."

Fig. 2-6. This ornamental gas postlight, once considered quaint, has suddenly become obsolete and a source of much irritation and unexpected expense with rising gas prices. Tenants are also beginning to resent the fact that they are paying to light up the streets at night, and on a 24-hour basis because the gas lights burn perpetually. Who needs a light in the daytime?

Who Pays For Street Lighting?

"All the parks have street lighting, but not the same kind. Some provide their own mercury vapor street lights with the park paying the bill for electricity. In others the tenants pay to light the streets on a 24-hour basis. The parks install an ornamental type postlight in front of every home which burns gas (Fig. 2-6). The three gas mantels in this lightburn forever, with the tenant paying for the gas—and who needs a gaslight in the daytime? Drive through one of these parks at night and you will find over half of these street lights turned off by the owners as a protest. Most of the lights which are still burning will give off little light because mantels are broken by moths and insects. As a result, streets in these parks are dark, inviting vandalism."

THE PARK OFFICE

"All three-plus parks are supposed to have an official office in the park, as required by state law and to keep their national rating. Some do, some don't. The finest park in this tri-state area has an office which is open only five days a week, 9 to 5, doing nothing but collecting the rent. Every Friday evening, the manager and his office assistant vanish for the weekend. If you phone, you get a recorded message which instructs you to leave your name and state your problem. When he heard this message for the first time, one park tenant gave his name and said: 'My problem is *you!*'

"This man told me, 'An office that is here just to collect the rent is like no office at all. They could rent a post office box and collect the rent through the mail. I'm going to move as soon as I can save the money.'

"Why is an office so important to you?' I asked him.

"He said, 'To stand as a symbol of law and order, just like the Roman fasces and six bundles of rods. This old Roman symbol of authority, plus a handful of men, was all that was needed to maintain law and order in nations of millions. But this symbol is meaningless without a human presence, and I don't mean a recorded telephone message. In the evenings, and on weekends when the office is empty, this park becomes a jungle and that's quoting the chairman fo the Township Trustees, who says 'some mobile home parks are a pain in the neck to the community, accounting for 56 out of 177 police calls received by the new township police force.'

"That's what happens when you have no office or manager to enforce the rules,' he said. 'All we got here is a high school dropout who moves his lips when he reads comic books all day. For this he even has a secretary to help him collect the rent so he doesn't have to stop reading and dog-ear a page. The park rules are ten times more effective in maintaining law and order than those clowns in the township police department. They just ride over here with their clipboards and make out a report, which makes them look good statistically, justifies their existence and gives the township trustees leverage when they ask for new tax levies. The park office has the power to invoke the Kiss of Death—eviction!'

"As you can see," Garrison said to me, "all things are not equal in mobile home land, even if they all do have the same national star ratings. You still have to personally check every park, personally see and talk to every manager, preferably in his office during working hours."

"Why in his office?" I asked.

"To see how he behaves when he answers the telephone. Even though his office assistant takes most of the hundreds of call received every day, some are still referred to him. That's why so many managers hate to live in the park. That's why that other manager had an unlisted telephone number—to get away from the constantly ringing telephone and the park's problems. Some managers can handle this with grace. Most can not.

"In the office, you will have a good opportunity to observe firsthand how the manager reacts because the telephone will never stop ringing while you are there. And he will be forced to take a few of the calls. Watch him closely, note the expression on his face, the comments he makes when he hangs up. Of he says, 'That old witch is always complaining,' then you will have problems if you move your home into that park—expensive problems, like moving."

"Why?" I asked.

"Some day your wife will call him to complain about some kids trespassing, pulling crabapples off your tree and throwing them at homes. And the manager will say the same thing about your wife."

I was glad I had persisted in tracking down Garrison and talking with him. Our little chat saved me a lot of misery and money.

3

Save On
The Right Lot

When I questioned a Michigan park manager about a good lot, he snapped, "What do you mean good lot? All our lots are good lots. You don't even have to go out there and look at them. You can pick one right off this plat drawing; and if you want to save money, don't pick a corner lot. The corners cost more."

"How much?"

"Ten bucks a month."

"Why?"

"They're bigger and you get one less neighbor to fight with."

"Then they're better and I oughta go look."

"You'll be wasting your time. They're all rented."

"How come? You just opened this park."

"Everybody wants a corner, nobody wants to save money. I wish we could build a park with nothing but corners. All we got left is regular lots, and they're all the same, like beans in a bucket. You can see for yourself on that map."

I looked. He was right. On a black and white line drawing they all *did* look alike, but if you ever hear anything like that, don't believe it because the lots are *not* all good locations. They may look equal on that big plat drawing in the manager's office, with all the red, yellow and blue thumbtacks, but some are more equal than others.

THE LOTS ARE NOT ALL EQUAL

Nick and Veronica T., who live in a 70 × 14 Fleetwood, believed it when they heard that all inside lots were equal, and now

Nick is complaining bitterly to Consumer's Power about his "fantastic" electric bill for the month of July.

In that one month it zoomed to $78 from a previous average of $26. Friends of theirs, Steve and Mary K., who also lived in a 70 × 14 Fleetwood, with the same size and make of air conditioner, only had a bill of $32 covering the same period and the same number of days. So there just *had* to be something wrong with the meter, Nick told the Consumer's Power office in Monroe.

The manager, who hears this many times, would usually have given Nick the polite brushoff routine because the meters are almost never at fault for sudden large billings and to check out every complaint would be an enormous waste of time, manpower and money. But this was a bad time for utility companies. They were being attacked on all sides by environmentalists, consumers, the press, questioned by congressional committees and hit with new regulations by federal agencies. So the manager just groaned

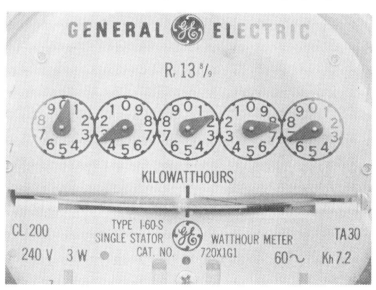

Fig. 3-1. Learn how to read your mobile home's electric meter and monitor your daily Kilowatt Hour usage. Read each dial from left to right and record the number each hand has just passed. On the dial above, the reading is 3176. If on the previous day the meter had read 3150, then 26 KWH have been used in the last 24 hours. To determine your KWH rate, check your last bill and divide its cost by the number of Kilowatt Hours used. Using this rate, you can calculate the cost of your electricity over any given time period. You can further use this calculation to find out what is making your bill so large. Experiment, turning things off for a day at a time, and see what makes the most difference in your usage.

inwardly, put on his best public relations smile and said he would have the meter checked.

A few days later, a service man came and wasted no time checking anything, he just put in a brand new General Electric meter (Fig. 3-1).

So what happened? The next month, an unusually hot and sunny August, Nick's electric bill increased another five dollars to a staggering $83 while his friend Steve's bill was still only $32.

The manager of Consumer's Power tried to calm Nick by promising to have the matter thoroughly investigated. If the company was at fault, the bill would be adjusted.

The Consumer Power generating plant is on the western shore of Lake Erie, a mere five miles away from Nick's mobile home park. One of the company's bright young engineers also lived in that same park with his new bride. The manager asked him to make a survey of the situation. He did, and this is his official report:

MEMO TO: JBC
FROM: BBN
SUBJECT: Residential service overcharge to mobile home in RAINBOW VILLAGE, 207 Daisy Lane.

Now G.E. meter, Type I-60-S, single stator, catalogue No. 720-X-1G1, installed 8/2/1975. Meter functioning properly 9/5/1975. Zero resistance, no service load, 125 volts no load at all wall outlets, 250 volts no load at air conditioner and electric range service outlets. Meter recording 4 KWH per hour.

Explanation for excessive KWH usage is the lot location on which this mobile home sits. This home is a single wide and is on a north/south lot, and has no awnings or carport. Home presents a 70 foot surface of metal to the morning sun. There is also an additional 1,000 sq. ft. of uncoated sheetmetal on the roof and 112 sq. ft. of unprotected picture window on the home front which faces directly south. In the afternoon, home presents the same surface area of metal to the west sun.

All drapes and curtains in this home are always kept drawn to admit sunlight because owner firmly believes this is beneficial because it kills germs and is generally healthful. Thermostat is set at 70 degrees. Air conditioner runs constantly with few off cycles. Home has three entrances, but no storm doors. Storm windows have been removed and there is leakage around many windows, a type which can be cranked open from inside.

The Fleetwood home at 118 Fox Run, with the more normal billing which I was also asked to check, is identical in size and design to the home at 207 Daisy Lane. But there the similarity ends. The Fox Run home sits on an east/west lot with the driveway on the southern exposure. There is a 70 foot carport over this driveway, which protects the entire south exposure of the home from the sun, and eliminates the need for awnings. The east and west exposures of the home are shaded by good awnings and heavy drapes which are kept closed during the day. All storm windows were left in, all doors have additional storm doors with glass instead of screens.

The roof on this home was painted with two coats of an extremely white mobile home roof coating and could actually be sat on in the noon sun without discomfort. The thermostat here was set at 76 degrees, the recommended temperature for comfort and economy. Air conditioner runs at normal 50/50 on/off cycles. The meter in this home was recording considerably less than 2 KWH usage.

The Consumer's Power office mailed Nick a copy of this report, and again he went beserk with rage. Even though Nick is pugnacious when angered, he is not stupid. He just verbally abused the manager for neglecting to tell him the true facts when he came to inquire about renting a lot. This led to a further interchange of insults, with Nick finally demanding that he be moved, without cost, to another lot. When he was told where to go, he left with the threat that he would sue.

THE TRUE FACTS ABOUT LOTS

Although Nick never did sue, he did consult a lawyer, which cost him a few bucks and further added to his great unhappiness because, as he remarked to a neighbor, "How the hell was I to know that it made a big difference which direction a mobile faced? I thought those lots were all alike."

This is pretty much what the troubled manager of a park in Minnesota told a state legislative committee investigating consumer complaints of bad practices in mobile home parks. He said, "All the lots in my park, except those on corners, are priced the same because they *are* the same. The fact that some lots bring the homeowner problems with mice, or other petty annoyances like noise or blowing dust, is not something I should be expected to know anymore than a real estate salesman should know that a certain area might flood in heavy rains. What *might* happen in any area is irrelevant and not for me to anticipate. I don't hide anything. The lots in my park are all right out there in the open. You can examine them as often as you please."

The park manager was right. Nick admitted that he had picked his lot directly off that big plat map in the manager's office (Fig. 3-2).

PICKING A LOT OFF THE OFFICE MAP

It had been a cold wet day, a sharp wind was blowing off the lake and Nick was in a hurry because he had to go to work. There were only about 30 lots left anyway, so he had just selected one that was close to the park's central antenna because he had been told that the further you were from the antenna, the poorer the reception.

Nick's friend Steve told me, "I tried to warn Nick about that lot. I told him his home would be hot in the summer if he took that lot, and he said, 'You sound like that Detroit sports writer who wrote that the hot August sun would be a factor in the All Stars football game with the Steelers. Paul Brown once said that the sun shines on both sides of the scrimmage line, and I'm saying that the sun shines on *all* the lots in this park. My home's gonna get hot no matter where I put it. Besides, I already made a deposit and stuck a yellow thumbtack in that wall map. That means *sold*.' "

Changing Your Mind On A Lot

"And I said, 'You can always change your mind and move that lousy thumbtack to another lot. You can change your mind up 'til the day your home arrives and they set it up on the lot. After that, it'll cost dough to change your mind.' "

Steve shook his head. I didn't try to tell him about his driveway. He found out later after the home was all set up—and did he blow his top! You could hear him swearing a block away."

"What did Nick find out about the driveway?" I asked.

"It was on the wrong side of the house (Fig. 3-3), which is what happens when you pick a lot off the map."

A mobile home salesman in Detroit told me, "A great many buyers study the plat drawing in the warm, comfortable park offices, select a lot, then just drive past it for a quick look as they are leaving. On a cold wet spring day, with the ground soft and muddy, who wants to get out of the car? Besides, the lots all look alike. But they are *not* all alike, as they later find out. The plat drawing does not indicate the position of driveways or patio slabs."

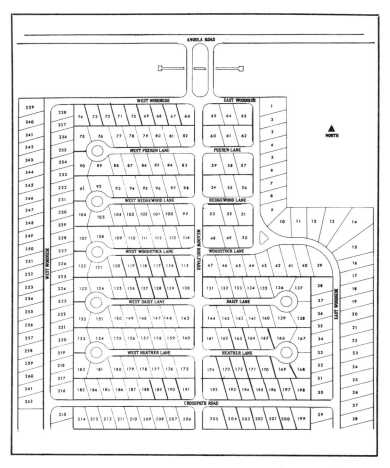

Fig. 3-2. This is a typical mobile home park plat drawing that you will see on the wall of every park manager's office. It will be filled with colored thumbtacks. The corner lots will almost always have a thumbtack stuck in them, indicating they are unavailable. Note that the drawing tells you nothing about the lot other than its number and location.

I was surprised to discover that the mobile home of the young engineer for Consumer Power also sat on a north/south lot, just like Nick's. Anticipating my question, he said, "Yes, I have a large electric bill, too. So why did I, with all my knowhow, select this lot? I didn't. I got married and started my new job on practically the same day. We bought this home in Detroit. I had a million things on my mind, so my wife came here alone and picked out a lot. It was a miserable, cold day and it was so easy, she said, to just push a thumbtack into a wall map. Our home was shipped from Detroit that same week, and by the time I saw the lot, it was too late. Besides, big electric bills don't bother me because my employers make the stuff."

A Mistake Anybody Can Make

"Picking the wrong lot is a mistake anybody can make, even an engineer's wife.

"Would it be worth the expense to move to another lot?" I asked.

"No," he said quickly. I figured it out one night with a calculator. We would have to continue living here at least another 15 years to recover our moving costs from savings on the electric bill. And we don't expect to be here that long."

Jack D., foreman of mobile home set-up crew for Community Developers, Inc., told me, "There are so many things to think about when picking out a lot, and when people do start thinking, it's too late."

"What is there to think about?" I asked.

DO THE LOT AND HOME FIT EACH OTHER?

He said, "Take a good look at those lots across the street. Do you notice anything different about any of them?"

I studied them a moment. They all looked exactly alike except some had more weeds, and some were covered almost entirely with sand. I mentioned this.

"Don't you see anything *else*?" he persisted.

I looked again. "Nope," I said.

Where Is The Driveway?

"Now perhaps you'll understand why so many people get hurt financially when they have to spend about $500 to have another door put in their homes (Fig. 3-4) on the driveway side. Look again now. Those driveways are *not* all the same. Some are on the right. But on the corner lot, the driveway is on the left."

Where Is The Patio Slab?

"Now look at those patio slabs. Most are on the left. On the corner lots, the patio is on the right. Suppose your home has an expando or tag on the right, but most of the driveways are on the right and you'll be parking your car on the front porch. The expando or tag should be foundationed on the patio slab, but this is on the *left*."

70

Fig. 3-3. This is what Nick saw when his home was delivered. The driveway was on the right, but his entrance door was on the left. When a carport was installed, his wife still had to walk through snow and rain to get the groceries into the house. Information like this cannot be seen on park plat drawings.

Where Is The Entrance Sidewalk?

"If the tag and porch are on the left, then the entrance sidewalk should also be on the left, otherwise your sidewalk is running right into the front of your home and ruining your shrubs and flowers. It looks awful. Drive through the park and notice all the sidewalks which go nowhere. Notice all the driveways on the wrong side of the house. You spend two thousand bucks for a carport, then you have to walk 100 feet through rain and snow to an entrance door on the opposite of the home. You'd be amazed at how many people there are who find out these things *after* their home is set up on the wrong lot. Then they wail and cry and blame the park, which starts them off with a very bad relationship, especially when they have to spend another thousand bucks. If you want to really save money when you buy a mobile home, be sure the lot and home fit each other. Be sure everything you need is there."

"Like what else?" I asked.

IS ANYTHING MISSING?

"Be sure that nothing is missing—that everything is in the right place, especially water and sewage. The water risers, those columns of drainage tile buried in the ground where the incoming water line emerges, are not all installed in a uniform pattern or in the same place. Some will come up under your home close to the connection, some will be outside the home and quite a distance from the connection. This is bad for many reasons. It doesn't look good, must eventually be camouflaged, and there is more pipe to protect with heat tape so the water won't freeze."

Too Long A Sewage Line

"If the sewage connection is in the wrong place, this will lengthen the piping required. The longer the pipe, the less the drop. With front kitchens this can cause all kinds of problems with clogged drains. Ideally, the sewage connection should be about in the middle so as to make all tap-ins from the kitchen, utility room and two bathrooms short as possible, 20 feet being the maximum length for any single run."

Clogged Drains

"We set up a front kitchen Croydon last winter on a lot where the sewer came up at the extreme back end, right by the electric meter. The sewer line from the kitchen sink was 60 feet long, with

Fig. 3-4. This mobile home owner also found out too late that his driveway was on the wrong side, and finally had a new door installed a year later at a cost of $595. Had this owner known about the driveway, he could have rented another lot. Alternatively, the home manufacturer (if notified in time) could have moved the location of the door at little or no cost.

only a two foot drop over that entire distance. Well, within three weeks they had a clogged drain in the kitchen. That poor woman was sick because she had to stop using her garbage disposal, and it was the garbage disposal that caught her eye in the first place. She had never had a garbage disposal."

ANCHORS AND FOUNDATIONS

"Notice anything else about those lots?" he asked.

I looked around again. In the vastness of that large empty section of the park, all I could see were rows of electric meter boxes, strips of blacktop driveways and concrete patio slabs. It all blended together into a glob. So I just shrugged.

He said, "Didn't you notice those steel loops in the concrete ribbons? Anchoring of mobile homes is now required by state law and that's what those steel loops are for. But anchoring loops are not provided for the big tag additions or one half of the doubles. The tag and *both* halves of a double should be anchored."

Auger Type Anchors

"In many three star parks, they don't provide a ribbon foundation for the home. Your home is set directly on the ground. But all better parks provide either a concrete slab foundation or ribbons, which eliminates the need for those auger anchors which are screwed into the ground. This has to be done before the home is put on the lot because you can't crawl under the floor and do this later. Those anchors are about four feet long and you just don't have the working space."

Building Block Foundations

"The majority of parks around here set up homes on building blocks, either directly on the ground, or on a cement foundation. Building blocks are hollow and have a poor bearing surface if put directly on the ground. They can crack, or even collapse. They also sink in the ground during freezes and thaws. If it were my home, I would insist on solid cement footing blocks, with the big 16-inch square blocks directly on the ground, followed by the smaller 8 × 16 blocks. The 16-inch blocks won't sink or settle and they provide a pretty good foundation."

Half Cement/Half Ground Foundations

"If you're buying a home with a tag, or a double, beware of half cement/half dirt foundations. This can mean expensive troubles. The half of your home that is foundationed directly on the ground will eventually sink and pull away from the half that is foundationed on cement. The two halves of your home are usually held together at the bottom and top by nothing more than 8-inch lag screws.

"When the tag (or half of a double) starts to settle, that's when you've got troubles. The least little movement will break the caulking seal on the roof and then you'll begin to see those ugly brown stains on the ceiling where the water has leaked in."

DRAWBACKS TO THE BIG HOMES

"That is one of the reasons why I didn't buy a bigger home myself. I didn't think that extra few square feet of living space was worth the cost and the troubles. You've got more space to heat and cool. You've got lots more maintenance. You've got more problems and expenses if you ever have to move. Another thing, all good parks provide a cement foundation—but *only* for single wides. I haven't seen one yet that provided a full foundation with steel anchor loops for the big new doubles. The best parks furnish a cement slab for the utility building, but only for the small 9 × 7 size. If you get the optional 10 × 10 building, the slab is too small. You always find *this* out at the last minute, while the building is being assembled. Nobody ever thinks to measure that slab before they order a larger building. There are so many little things like this to think about, I could write a book."

THE NEW CONCEPT IN CARE-FREE LIVING

Virginia T., a working widow who lives alone in a big Croydon, told me, "I rented a lot in this park because they cut the grass and shovel the snow. 'This is the new concept in care-free living,' the manager told me. 'We even have a private section for adults only.' "

"A nice section, quiet with no kids. I liked that," Virginia said. "I'm on my feet all day, I'm tired when I get home, my feet hurt and I don't want to be bothered every day clearing toys and tricycles out of my driveway before I can park my car. So every day now I have to stop out in the street and remove something from my driveway before I can park. You know why? I made the dumb mistake of selecting this lot right on the boundary line of the adult section, and the west boundary of the park. My next door neighbor has four little pre-school children. Nobody told me about that boundary line. I thought I was in the middle of the adult section. Not that it would make any difference because children don't know anything about boundaries. They're all over the park anyway. Adult sections are a big joke. It sounds good when the manager tells you about it."

What's Next To The Park

"I figured on the west boundary of the park I would have no neighbors behind me, just an 8-foot chain link barbwire fence. That was another dumb mistake. Beyond that fence are 50 acres of weeds and sand—perfect for motorcycle racing in the summer, and snowmobiles in the winter. In addition to the noise, there's the sand which the prevailing westerly winds blow in my direction. In the fall, mice, rabbits and rats come out of that field and head for the crawl space under the mobile homes along that western boundary and fence. They never cross the street to go beyond us because nobody else in the park has troubles with vermin under their homes. Just we who live on the boundary next to that field."

The Middle Section Is Best

"I'm not the only tenant here who regrets making the dumb mistake of renting a lot around the outer edge just to avoid having a neighbor in back. The trouble is we have no idea what might someday be along that outer edge. This is country out here.

Somebody might buy that 50 acres next to me to store junk cars. If I had it to do over, I'd pick a lot right in the middle of the adult section, or right in the middle of the park. That way I'd be surrounded by adults and far enough away from the outer boundaries so that motorcycles and snowmobiles wouldn't bother me."

The Corner Lots

"What do you think about corner lots?" I asked.

"You can have them!" she said quickly.

"They eliminate one neighbor also..."

"They also cost more to rent. They're larger which means more grass to cut."

"So what? The park cuts it."

"The park butchers it! They cut my grass once. Never again! They don't catch the grass clippings, or rake them. They wait too long to cut, the grass is high and they cut it too short, with the dead clippings making your lawn look like a hay field. Cutting grass too short in hot, dry weather kills it. In the summer you can tell which lawns the park cut because they are the ones that are all brown and dead. We call them 'lawn butchers.' All the good lawns in this park are owner maintained. That 'carefree living concept' is just a bunch of garbage. I work harder here than my husband did when we owned our home with half an acre."

"You sound like you don't like it here," I remarked.

"I wouldn't go that far. Let's just say that I would like it a lot better if I had known what I was doing when I picked out my lot, and I would have saved a lot of money which I couldn't afford to spend."

"How?"

"By not being forced to spend an extra $2000 to completely enclose my carport on all sides to keep out the kids. By not being forced to spend another $200 to have all the piping openings under my home sealed off with aluminum to keep out the mice and rats."

"Do you still have trouble with children?"

"Not if I keep the carport gates locked. But that creates another problem for me. My air conditioning compressor and condenser are under the carport and it gets very hot under there, like over 100 degrees. If only I had known, all the money I could have saved."

"Is there anything *good* about the lots in this park?" I asked.

She had to think a moment. "It's really a nice place, except for that dumb manager. The water and sewage are free. I don't like that gas post lantern. The mantels are always being broken by bugs, and they cost 50 cents each. Because of the gas shortage, most of the people here are turning their lights off. So when a committee complained to management about the dark streets, they were told that if the park installed mercury vapor street lights, it would mean a rent increase."

"Why don't you convert to electricity?" I asked.

Converting The Gas Lights

"Some of the people here are doing that. I would if it didn't cost so much."

"How much?"

"Some man in a van stopped last week and offered to do the job. He wanted $250 for a regular incandescent conversion with a utility outlet on the post. He wanted $350 for a mercury vapor conversion and photo electric eye to switch the light on and off. I wish I could do it myself."

PARKING PROBLEMS

The custom-built Landola Joe and Marge K. bought two years ago in Columbus, Ohio has been adequate for their needs. They wish they could say as much for the parking space that came with their lot. It holds two cars, yes, but one back of the other. This creates problems, like car juggling. Joe comes home from work after Marge, but she leaves for work in the mornings before he does. This means switching the cars around before going to bed. The problem was soon compounded when Joe Jr. reached his 18th birthday, went to work, and bought his own car. The park does not permit parking on the street, except for overnight guests.

This is another thing which the prospective lot renter should look into very closely, even to using a tape measure, because mobile homes lots may rent equally in price, and may even look equal, but some are more equal than others.

When you start to measure with a tape, you will find some driveways long enough to hold three cars, one behind the other. Then not too far away you will find another driveway just barely long enough to take one full size car before you drive over the utility building foundation. Some parks use a single wide driveway which is shared by two homes. This makes installing a carport almost impossible.

Joe solved the parking problem for son Joe Jr., but it was costly. He had the steel utility building disassembled, and moved back 15 feet. Since the 10 × 10 slab was higher by six inches than the blacktop driveway, it had to be broken up and removed. Then another cement slab had to be poured for the utility building, and 15 feet of the driveway blacktopped. Joe's driveway can now hold three cars, but it cost him almost $1,000. And the daily car juggling game has now become even more of a problem.

If you're buying a mobile home to save money, this is *not* the way.

THE ENTRANCE AND KICKBACK FEES

Many good parks will not rent you a lot until you pay an "entrance fee." This can be as much as $500. Some also charge an "exit fee." I will explain later how they can force payment of this fee. The justification for these fees, one park owner explained, is that it cost him over 3 million dollars to develop raw land into a decent modern community of 400 lots for mobile home living. This, he said, figured out at $7500 per lot, and he could not recover this with rentals alone.

Many parks also require anyone doing business on their property to kick back about 10 percent of their charges. This could be for anything from a pizza or Chicken Delight delivery to a $2,000 carport or awning installation. The service people, usually only a favored few, simply add this kickback to their charges. This means that a $2,000 carport costs $2,200 in that particular mobile home park.

There is legislation pending in some states to ban entrance fees and kickbacks and by the time this is printed, it may already be illegal in your state. But in many states it is still common practice. So investigate, and ask questions before you rent a lot in ANY park—especially those with high ratings because they represent huge capital investments and are run by professional hardnose managements who miss no angle for turning another buck.

The money-saving tip for all mobile homers looking for a lot is: *Don't* pick a lot off that big wall map in the manager's office, then give it a quick look as you drive past. Odds are it will cost you money if you do.

Save On 4
Heating And
Cooling Problems

Wanda and I took delivery of a Croydon the last week of July. It was hot and temperatures were in the high nineties. Immediately we understood why air conditioning is considered a high priority item in all mobile homes, even in the short—summer northern states along the Canadian border. In southern states, don't even *think* of living in a mobile home without air conditioning. Just like your automobile out in the sun, they really get hot inside—and it doesn't matter how much you stuff the walls with fiberglass insulation.

Although we had carefully selected an east/west lot with a long driveway, we were still sitting up on blocks with temporary wood steps, no skirting, no awnings or carport, the hitch still on. The air conditioner was running quite a bit, with only short off cycles. I didn't worry about this because I understood why and I figured it was only for a short time because Labor Day was only five weeks away. At least we were comfortable, I told Wanda.

At least for three days we were. Then it happened! The honeymoon ended on a sweltering Sunday afternoon. I was stacking books on shelves in my office when Wanda asked, "Do you feel warm?"

"Come to think of it, I do feel a little sticky. What's the thermometer say?"

She checked. "It's almost 80, and the thermostat is set for 76. Say, I haven't heard the air conditioner run for a while. Have you?"

The sound of air rushing up through the registers is hard to miss your first few days, and it *had* seemed rather quiet the last half hour. And since it was suddenly so quiet, we heard something else—a faint humming sound. We ran around trying to locate the source. I finally pinpointed it as coming from the air conditioner unit, which was partly underneath the tag addition where my office was located.

DON'T PANIC

The natural reaction is to panic or laugh when it happens to somebody else. A humming noise in a mysterious piece of equipment can be a frightening thing to the ignorant. Like Mark Twain once said, "Everybody's ignorant, only on different subjects." I'm ignorant on air conditioners.

I had enough sense left to turn the air conditioner off, which immediately stopped the humming, and I felt better.

"What do we do now?" Wanda asked.

Check the Manuals

I shrugged helplessly. Then I remembered something—the big Kraft envelope filled with papers, guarantees, and instruction manuals that came with the home. There were some papers on the Intertherm furnace and air conditioner. Sometimes in the manuals, like the ones that come with power lawnmowers, there is a troubleshooting chart. But not this time. Not a word about what to do if the air conditioner didn't run, but just hummed.

There was something else I found among those papers—a letter from the park office with a list of service companies who had been approved to do business in the park. On the list were two heating and air conditioning firms. Their services was available 24 hours a day, even on Sunday, and they had radio-dispatched trucks.

It sounded wonderful. So I called one of the firms and a recorded voice answered. *"Please specify the nature of your problem. Leave your name, address and telephone number. A service truck will be dispatched when available, usually within an hour."*

Who Pays For Service

"Can you *do* that?" Wanda asked timidly.

"Why?"

"Who's gonna pay for it?"

I thought a moment. "Me."

"How about the warranty? We've only been here three days."

"Intertherm's in St. Louis. Croydon's in Indiana. We're in Ohio. It's Sunday, it's hot."

"You're gonna pay for the service call?"

"What else?"

"Why?"

The Warranty Fine Print

"Did you ever read the fine print in a warranty? It says: 'The company shall not be liable for any labor costs.' That means service calls on Sunday."

"That's silly," Wanda said with typical female logic. "How can you fix anything without labor?"

"It's a long story." I said. "By the time I explain, it'll be winter and we won't need air conditioning."

One hour later, the temperature in our living room had passed the 90 mark. It was 94 outside. This was my first big disappointment—learning how quickly the inside temperature of a mobile home can approach the outside temperature, even with double insulation. The air conditioner had been off less than two hours, and we had closed all the drapes to keep out the sun. I wondered what it would have been like with just standard insulation in the walls.

My T-shirt was getting wet under the arms, so I said, "I'm going over to Montgomery Wards and buy a big fan. You stay here in case somebody comes."

"What good will a fan do?"

"I'll stick it in one of the back windows, open a front window and exhaust all the hot air and..."

"Pull in more hot air."

"It'll cool down outside," I said, leaving for the shopping center.

When I returned, the air conditioner was running, but the house was still warm. Wanda said, "The man just left. He said it would take a while to cool the house down again."

"How long was he here?"

"Mm, maybe five minutes."

"Just five munutes? What'd he do?"

"I don't know. He was kneeling on the ground. He removed a small plate, then he poked at something with a long red screwdriver, There was a loud clunk and the air conditioner came on."

"That's all?" I shouted.

"Well, no, he gave me a bill. I wrote out a check."

When I saw the bill, I almost had a heart attack. "Forty bucks!" I yelled. "And all he did was poke at something with a red screwdriver?"

"What could I do? I had to pay him."

Of course she was right, but I brooded about that forty dollars for days. I wondered about retirees in the park on fixed incomes, who were probably just making it with nothing left over at the end of the month. For them a forty dollar bill for just "poking at something" could be a disaster.

LOOK FOR MISTER FIX-IT

The weather cooled the next day and we had no more trouble with the air conditioner. So I tried out my new 10-speed racing bike. That's how I met Charley. A car passed me, I got too close to the curb and fell off the bike right in front of Charley's home. I felt foolish as he helped me up and offered to straighten my handlebars, which had been knocked off center when they hit the sidewalk.

We went back to his utility building workshop and I was amazed at what he had in that 10×10 space.

He was a garrulous, friendly man, like so many retirees are in mobile home communities. He had once been chief maintenance man for a big downtown office building. Now he was sort of an unofficial maintenance man in the park, a "Mister Fix-it" as some of the younger wives called him. Charley, I learned later, had an amazing knowledge of anything mechanical. He was the ultimate do-it-yourselfer. Nobody ever touched anything Charley owned, from the grass on his beautiful lawn to the watch on his wrist. If someday somewhere in this world a man performs do-it yourself brain surgery on himself, it will probably be Charley, or somebody like him.

There is a retired Charley in every mobile home community living out his life in loneliness and quiet desperation because the Charleys of this world just can't get used to doing nothing. So he fixes things, practically for nothing, just to be doing something, just to be around people because the young ones in the park shun him because he's old. They only remember Charley when they're in trouble and they come running to "Mister Fix-it." There is a Charley in your park. Be his friend and he will save you thousands of dollars. Forget that he is old, and he will never forget you.

When I told Charley about my air conditioner problem, and the forty dollar bill, he frowned, and said, "Well, ah, that's not really out of line. A regular week day service call is ten bucks just for ringing your doorbell. Then there's a minimum charge of another ten bucks for labor, which includes poking at something with a red screwdriver. Now, on Sunday these firms have double and triple time labor contracts. So, if you must have service on Sunday, you pay double the normal weekday rate. And don't blame them, blame the unions."

"How come you frowned, like something was wrong?" I asked.

"The ten dollar service charge is for driving 20 miles out here, but they were already here in the park when you called them. You weren't the only one who had air conditioner troubles last Sunday. There must have been a dozen homes that had the same humming problem. Every time we have a hot spell that company reaps a harvest in this park fixing air conditioners that don't have a bloody thing wrong with them."

"You mean I got shafted."

"Wait a minute! You did call for service on a Sunday. So you take the consequences. According to Murphy's law, if anything can possibly screw up, it will on Sunday night. There is some strange mysterious force in the universe that keeps furnaces, water heaters, garbage disposals, and air conditioners working perfectly during the normal work week of straight time pay. But from Saturday afternoon until Monday morning, when all the service people in the world vanish, air conditioners and furnaces stop running when you need them the most, sewer pipes clog up when you have a house full of guests.

"So you just pay up. But you said nothing was wrong with my air conditioner."

"That's right. You could just as easily have poked in there yourself and closed that relay."

THE LOW VOLTAGE PROBLEM

"Why didn't the relay close?"

"Low voltage. It happens all the time."

"Why? I'm paying for 240 volt service!"

"And you're getting it. I'm talking about momentary high surge voltage during peak load periods of the day, which is late in the afternoon when thousands of air conditioners are cycling on and off. You see, it's when a compressor cycles on that it causes problems with voltage. A 4-ton air conditioner will draw about 35 amps while running, but for one brief second, while getting started, it will draw ten times that much amperage. That's what is meant by high surge voltage drops. In the park here, over 75 per cent of the homes have air conditioning of some kind. That's a higher percentage than they planned for when this park was built. Now, normally this will not cause any troubles because air conditioners, refrigerators, and freezers don't all cycle on and off at the same split second. But, by the mathematical laws of probability, there will come a time when a whole bunch of compressors will cycle on at the same precise moment, and *that* is when you have a high surge voltage drop. Starter relays on air conditioners sometimes will not close when the voltage drops below 110. They just hang up in a halfway position and you get a humming sound. I checked the voltage in one of my wall outlets last Sunday and it was down to 102 volts at 5 p.m. An hour later it was back up to a normal 125 volts. When a starter relay hangs up, it's a simple matter to poke in there and push it down with a screwdriver like the service man did. That's what you can do yourself."

FIXING A STARTER RELAY

"How do I know what to poke?"

"Easy. You can *see* it. Remove the four hex-head sheetmetal screws on the cover plate over the electrical relay box. You can't miss it. It's that plate about 12 inches square on the right side. Have your wife turn the air conditioner on and off a few times while you watch carefully what happens in there. You will see something, move up and down with a loud clunk. When it snaps down, your compressor will come on. When it snaps up, the compressor will stop running. That thing that moves with a clunk is what you poke at with a screwdriver. You just barely touch it, and it will clunk, and the air conditioner will come on."

Don't Poke With Metal

"Can I use any old screwdriver?"

"No! The red screwdriver your wife saw the service man using was the insulated type used in TV alignment work. There's 240 volts in that box and you'll be kneeling on the ground. The safest thing to use is wood because it has zero conductivity. Personally, I always use a half inch dowel about 12 inches long. Don't use a wood ruler! They sometimes have a metal edge. Incidentally, I would suggest that when you replace that cover plate, use only one screw because you may have to go in there again before the season is over."

"How long will that go on?"

"Just for the rest of this heat wave. Like I said, they hadn't anticipated such a high percentage of air conditioned mobile homes, so they have a temporary transmission load problem

They're working to fix it right now with new lines and transformers. Next summer you won't have to do any poking into your relay."

I sighed. "What *else* can go wrong?"

"Very little. The compressors in air conditioners are sealed units, just like in refrigerators and freezers. They rarely cause trouble."

"Don't they ever have to be recharged?"

"They just replace the whole unit."

"How come my car air conditioner has to be recharged every year?"

"Automobile compressors are not sealed units. They are driven by V-belts off the engine. That pulley shaft into the compressor is the weak link. There's a nylon seal on that shaft, but the freon gas is sometimes under extremely high pressure, and it blows by that seal, especially after it drys out during the winter. That's why auto manufacturers recommend that during the winter you run your air conditioner once a week for a minute just to keep the seal lubricated. Do you do that during the winter?"

"I always forget."

"That's why you have to recharge every year. You're losing freon past that nylon seal."

OTHER PROBLEMS WITH AIR CONDITIONING

Something else went wrong with the air conditioning about two weeks later, but not with the unit itself. We were losing cooled air up the furnace chimney. Wanda noticed it while dusting. She asked my why "that metal pipe over the furnace is so cold and dripping wet."

I checked and was shocked to see water running down that ducting and laying in pools on the funace top—and the metal was so *cold*. I had also noticed the previous day that cold air coming up the floor register in the tag addition had for some strange reason diminished in velocity. Previously if a handkerchief were held over the register, it would wave and flutter like a flag in a stiff breeze. Now it barely moved. Something was wrong and I was baffled.

Wasted Air Conditioning

I went to see Charley and got a quick explanation as to what was wrong. Without any hesitation, he said, "It's your check valve."

"What the devil is that?" I said.

"Your furnace and air conditioner both use the same floor heat ducting. Check valves are in there Fig. 4-1 to prevent backflow. In your tag addition, two large flexible ducts, laying on the ground, tie into the floor heating system ductwork. One supplies heated air, the other cooled air. However, when one system is running, the other is closed off by a check valve. It prevents cooled air from backflowing to the furnace and up the chimney. In the winter it prevents warmed air from backflowing outside through the air conditioner. In your case, the check valve on the furnace side is stuck in the open position. You're losing better than 30 per cent of your air conditioning up the chimney. In the winter, you waste the same amount of heat."

"Is it hard to fix?" I aked, anticipating another big service call.

"Not at all. It's very easy to fix, in a messy, uncomfortable sort of way because you have to crawl through weeds and dirt dragging along a tool box and trouble light to the duct work under your tag. That's why you should never throw away old trousers, shirts and shoes because they come in handy for working under your home. Personally, I prefer coveralls because there is no belt area around your waist for dirt to work into, and your pants don't keep coming down as you crawl in a forward direction."

"Sounds like fun," I said.

"I'm probably making it sound a lot worse than it really is. The hardest part is crawling to the furnace entry under the tag. After you're there, the rest is easy. You remove the flexible ducting, which is secured very loosely, if at all, with 2-inch aluminum duct tape. With the flexible duct removed, you can see the check valve. It's nothing but a 10-inch flap of metal, usually something light like aluminum so it can be easily raised or closed by air flow. It is loosely hinged and rarely ever sticks. When it does, it's usually because some careless workman left something under the flap, like a tool. I found a pair of pliers under one once. After you've cleaned out the area, remove the obstruction, put a dab of grease on the hinge, and make sure it opens and closes easily and tightly. You may have to remove that short strip of sponge rubber put there to deaden sound when the flap drops. That strip of ¼-inch rubber prevents a tight closing of the flap, and leaves a considerable opening for leakage. I removed it from mine for that reason. I'd rather have the noise than the leakage."

"That doesn't sound too hard," I said.

"It isn't. So while you're underneath there, you might as well check a few other things, like whether the flexible ducts are

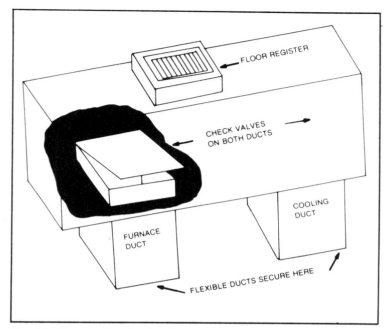

Fig. 4-1. The check valve flap is made of very light metal so air flow pressure can open or close it. The air flow from the furnace opens this flap and at the same time closes the flap opposite on the cooling side. This prevents heat from backflowing out through the air conditioner.

properly secured at both ends. As you will find out, working under a mobile home is painfully uncomfortable, which is why I wear extra clothing under my coveralls as padding to cushion the inpact of all those sharp stones and bumps in the ground. I also wear a beret on my head to keep burrs and dead grass out of my hair. It's the ideal thing to wear because it doesn't keep falling off or get in your way. People kid me about my basque beret but it makes a lot more sense than a hat.

WHY YOUR GAS BILL IS SO HIGH

"You will quickly understand," Charley said, "why home set-up crews, those kids with transistor radios taped to one ear, waste no time working under homes. It's sheer agony and they hate it. That's why they rush through the work and that's why it is often so badly done. Yet, what is done *under* a home is the most important part of the set-up. Don't be surprised if you find one of the flexible ducts, either at the furnace or air conditioner end, hanging lose with only a piece of tape holding it to the metal duct. This will explain why it is either unusually warm in the winter or cool in the summer under your home. This will explain why your furnace never stops running and why you have a gas bill of $75 while your neighbor, with the same space to heat, only has a bill for $32. You are heating the crawl space."

"Does that happen often?" I asked.

"In this park, I'd say half the homes."

"Good grief!" I shouted. "No wonder there's a gas shortage."

"Wait a minute now. When I said half the homes. I was referring only to the doubles. It is only in these homes that you have big flexible ducting lying on the ground to carry heat over to the tag or other half of a double. In single wides with expandos and tipouts this isn't necessary because the existing metal ducting under the floor is all that is needed to distribute the heat and air conditioning."

Don't Heat The Crawl Space

"My home has a big tag."

"And your home has flexible ducts," Charley said quickly. Check them. Don't heat the crawl space. Whenever anyone complains to me about their heating or air conditioning costs, the first thing I suggest is that they check those ducts. Most of the time, that will be the cause. And you will understand why when you yourself, working alone in a tight crawl space, try to hold and tape one of those squirming beasts to a metal floor duct. It's like trying to put a greased pig into a plastic bag. It takes one pair of hands just to cut and manage the sticky duct tape."

How to Secure The Flexible Duct

"The flexible ducts consist of three parts: an inner spiral coil of tough springy wire, a middle 1-inch layer of insulation, and an outer layer of thin, brittle plastic cover which you can puncture or tear with a dirty look. As you slide the end of this unmanageable mess over the furnace fitting and tape it, the inner layers of insulation and coiled wire immediately slide down and only the outer plastic cover is secured to the furnace fitting. Eventually it tears and the flexible duct winds up hanging half on, half off. That is how the job is done by those kids with the transistor radios. That is why you will probably be heating the crawl space this winter.

"How do I prevent this?" I asked.

"By securing that inner coil of wire to the furnace fitting and not just with duct tape," Charley said. "First, you drill four holes into the furnace fitting, then into those holes you screw four hex-washer head sheetmetal screws, driving them in only half way. The inner coil of wire you now slide up over those washer-head screws, letting one strand of the wire rest on the screws behind the washer. Tighten all four screws over the wire. The insulation material and the outer plastic cover you now slide up over the screws and secure with the duct tape. This flexible duct now will never drop off or come loose.

"Why don't the set-up crews do it that way?" I asked.

Charley gave me a disgusted look. "If you were a kid, would you go to all that bother, unless someone was supervising and ordered you to? Most of the time these kids are working without any supervision. They're working under very disagreeable conditions and they're in a hurry to get out from under your home.

"How nice," I said. "So what else is fouled up?"

"You might check your sewer lines, the long one from the front kitchen or bathroom, and the short one back in the middle. That middle sewer line is rarely ever a problem because it's short and has a good drop.

SEWER LINE PROBLEMS

"The long sewer line, especially if you have a front kitchen, can be trouble because there is often 50 or more feet to travel with little drop—or worse yet, a dip and a rise in the line. The line never drains completely of water or garbage.

"The set-up crews, working hurriedly usually hang this sewer pipe to cross trusses with nothing more than throw-away 18-gauge copper wire that came with your home's temporary travel light system. You can break one of these supports of the pipe by resting your arm for a moment on the pipe. I know because I did this."

Sewer Line Dips

"If your long sewer line has a dip, I strongly advise you to straighten it out before that dip fills up with coffee grounds; they have a nasty way of settling in low spots or building up in elbows. Coffee grounds can clog a sewer drain faster then anything except diapers."

This scared me because my sewer line *did* have a dip right in the middle. When I mentioned this, he said, "You now have a valid reason to replace all that junk wire that was used on your sewer line. You can level off as you do this."

Charley was right. Throw-away tail-light wire had been used to hold up my pipe.

"Should I replace the wire with hanger strap?" I asked.

Don't Use Hanger Strap...

"You can, but I personally prefer the solid type aluminum clothesline wire. It's an absolute joy to work with, easy to cut, bend and tie. It's also very strong, will not rust and can be re-used if you ever move. Hanger strap will additionally require two ¼-inch bolts at each support. It will rust and it won't be easy to bolt at the precise degree of tightness because two holes in the strap will not always line up exactly where you want. And again you have a dip. You want that sewer pipe to lie perfectly straight with a slow gradual drop—as much drop as the crawl space will allow. Aluminum clothesline wire is the cheapest, easiest, fastest way to get the job done, and done right. Hanger straps and bolts will get rusty and be very difficult to remove—and when they are removed, you'll just throw the whole mess away. So do it the easy was—buy two coils of solid aluminum clothesline wire at any hardware store. It also comes in a braided wire that's painted so it won't soil clothes, but you don't want that. The solid, uncoated stuff is better."

I sighed. "Anything else?"

THOSE FLOOR HOLES

He thought for a moment. "Yeah. While you're still under the house laying on your back with a rock pressing against your hip bone wondering how you ever got into such a stupid position, you better check the floor holes.

"Holes!" I shouted.

"The four entry points for sewer, water and gas. Depending on the manufacturer, this job is done either neatly or sloppily. I have seen huge jagged holes that looked like they were hacked out with a fire ax. If you leave these over-size holes uncovered, you could have problems with little animals like mice and rats. You will also have gnats, flies, mosquitoes, and crickets. If your wife has been complaining about gnats and flies getting in the house, you have holes to cover.

"Another overlooked point of entry for gnats and flies is the air vent for your gas hot water heater. It's in the floor of the tiny room with the outside door. Air for combustion is supplied through a short length of round downspouting which extends about 18 inches down into the crawl space. The crawl space, incidently, is a haven for insects, and helps them survive past the first frost. I have seen flies and mosquitoes buzzing around my worklight when it was snowing outside. If you don't cover all points of entry, you could have a big fly buzzing through your home, driving you crazy on Christmas day."

"Do they come up through the floor holes?" I said.

"Yes, but mostly through that vent pipe in the hot water compartment because it's warm in there. You also have a big hole in the wall here for the water lines which will look like it was hacked out by some demented volunteer fireman. This hole can be big enough for a cat to walk through. This is how insects get from the hot water compartment into the bathroom, and then through your home to drive your wife crazy because she thinks they're getting in around the screen doors. So she keeps yelling at you to fix the doors."

I smiled because this was true. Wanda had been nagging me about the flies and I had accused her of holding the door open too long when she brought in the groceries. "How do you keep the insects from getting in the hot water compartment?" I asked.

Cover the vent hole in the floor with *two* layers of screen material. One layer will keep out flies, but not the gnats. You have four additional holes under your home, plus the big one in the lower wall of the hot water compartment which must be sealed off. The best thing for this is sheet aluminum which you can buy in most hardware stores. Another similar item is flashing aluminum. This comes in rolls of various widths and lengths. It is easy to cut, even with ordinary scissors.

"For the ragged holes around the sewer pipe entrances, you will need 12 or 18 inch squares, depending on/how poorly the hole was cut. Directly in the center of each piece you draw, with a compass, a circle the exact diameter of the sewer pipe. You cut this out neatly by making one straight cut into the circle and then around to make the hole. This piece of aluminum sheet can now be worked around the pipe, then pressed up tight over the hole in the floor. You secure it with ½-inch sheetmetal screws. If you cut the right size hole, the fit will be tight enough to even keep out gnats. If your hole is too large, you can seal it off with Mortite, a rope-like caulking tape which comes in rolls. You just press it in around the pipe for a perfect air-tight seal. Do the same thing with the gas and water pipe entries.

"You won't be able to get as neat and tight a fit in the hot water compartment where copper tubing runs to the washbasins and shower. However, it doesn't have to be a perfect fit. Any gaping space around the tubing can later be filled with those odd pieces of fiberglass insulation you can find laying on the ground under your home. The important thing is to get that big, jagged partition hole covered to keep out stray animals.

"You will never again have troubles with mice, flies, gnats, mosquitoes or crickets. I think I hate crickets the worst. Like cockroaches, they eat anything."

"Won't mice make new holes?" I asked.

"No chance. The entire floor space under your home is filled with fiberglass, and mice just don't like the stuff. I guess it makes then sneeze."

Fiberglass makes me sneeze, too, or maybe it was the weeds under my home which I crawled over and lay on as I did all the things Charley told me about. Although my poor bones ached for days, it was worth the agony. No more wasted heat or air conditioning. No more clogged drains. No more flies or gnats.

For a few weeks, life in mobile homeland was serene, almost like it said in those park advertisements. Then came another crisis.

WIND AND YOUR PILOT LIGHT

It was a windy day in October. Wanda was washing clothes. There was panic in her voice when she called me at work. "We've got no hot water!"

This baffled me. Why do women panic when there's no hot water? I phoned Charley. He just laughed. "It's the wind. It blew out your pilot light."

I called Wanda back and told her. She wailed, "So what am I supposed to do?"

Why are women so dumb about pilot lights?

I called Charlie again. "Where the devil *is* the pilot light?"

"I'll show you when you get home," he laughed.

When I opened the door to my hot water compartment, Charley said, "Don't feel bad about not knowing how to relight a pilot light. You're not alone. That's why the service people make a bundle in this park every time we have high winds. They charge 20 bucks per call, 40 bucks on Sunday."

I gasped. "Why do winds affect pilot lights?"

"Small, short draft chimneys. It's only about 5 feet from the firebox to the roof. That makes pilot lights on mobile home furnaces and water heaters sensitive to high winds—and often in only one direction. That has always mystified me. For example, a

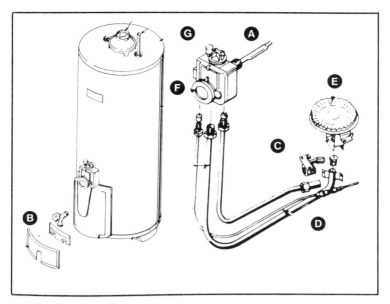

Fig. 4-2. The shut-off valve (A) must be closed (turn right) for five minutes before attempting to relight the pilot. Cover (B) must be removed. Pilot burner (C), heat sensor, or thermocouple (D), main burner (E), and thermostat (F) are also shown. The "push to light" button (G) must be held down at least 30 seconds after the pilot is lit.

25-mile-an-hour northeast wind will sometimes blow out my water heater pilot, but a 70-mile-an-hour gust from the southeast won't bother it. It blows out my furnace pilot instead. I'm still trying to figure out why. But in the meantime, I get out my special box of those long kitchen matches, and relight the pilot."

"How?" I asked.

Relighting Gas Pilots

"It's really very simple, but first let's look at what happens when a gas pilot flame is extinguished. You must understand this first to know what you're doing. That pilot flame has two functions: to ignite the main burners, and to send commands back to the thermostat under that small plastic cover (Fig. 4-2). The heat from that pilot flame is picked up by a heat sensor, which in turn sends commands back to the thermostat. If the pilot flame should go out, there would be no heat and the sensor would immediately send a command back to the thermostat to turn off the gas. Once the gas is turned off, it stays off.

"This is a safety device built into all gas heating equipment to protect you when the pilot is accidently extinguished. Without this protection, when your furnace would cycle on, the main burner would fill your home with gas. If this gas ever reached an open flame, like the pilots in your kitchen cooking range, you would never hear the loud noise because you would be half way to Philadelphia. This safety feature, however, has one serious drawback. If you should happen to be away for a few days, you could return to a cold home and frozen pipes. And that is the one big advantage of an electric burner in the furnace, instead of gas, because the electricity can go off for a few hours, but it always comes back on, and so does the furnace.

"Before proceeding to relight your pilot, I will need that long match holder which came with your furnace, and is probably lying on top of it. Will you get it, please?"

Charley was right. The match holder, a 24-inch length of metal with a clip device on end, was on my furnace. I had wondered what it was.

Charley took the match holder, then said, "Remove the plastic dust cover from the thermostat. Remove the panel at the bottom of the tank. The main burner and pilot are back in there. Turn the main gas valve clockwise, to right. Put one of these long matches on the end of this holder, light it, then, with your left finger pressing down on this push valve (Fig. 4-2), insert the lighted match way back into the firebox and you will suddenly see the pilot burning. *Don't* remove your finger from this push valve. If you do, the pilot flame will immediately go out again. You must hold this push valve down at least 30 seconds to give the heat sensor sufficient time to send a command back to the thermostat to open the gas.

"If, when you remove your finger from the push valve, the pilot keeps burning, the command was sent. If the pilot goes out, just repeat the same operation until the pilot stays on without your finger on that push valve.

"Now, the last step is to open that main valve. This time you turn counterclockwise, or left. But before you do this, put the cover back on the burner compartment while it is still cool. Later it will be too hot. When you open this main valve, you will immediately and clearly hear the burners come on with a roar. The job is finished and you have just saved yourself 20 bucks—or 40 bucks if you did this on Sunday."

Relighting the Furnace Pilot

"How about my furnace pilot?" I asked.

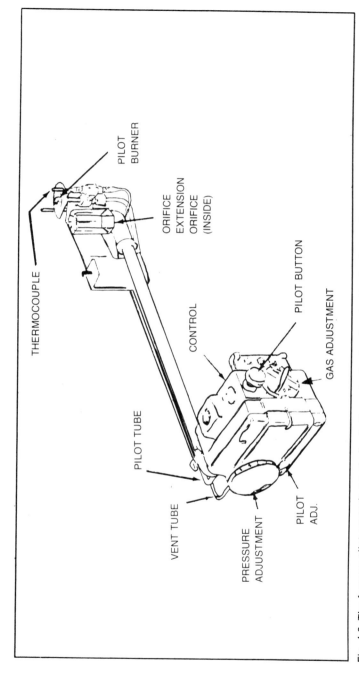

Fig. 4-3. The furnace pilot controls are similar to the water heater, they just look a little different. The relighting procedure to follow is exactly the same. The gas adjustment knob is the valve which is closed, and the pilot burner is pushed and held for at least 30 seconds.

95

"The relighting of a furnace pilot is basically the same routine, with a pilot push button and a main gas valve or adjustment (Fig. 4-3). The only difference is that in some furnaces you may have to remove a panel to get at the thermostat and valves. To get to your pilot burner, you lift that small weighted flap cover, which conceals a hole about three inches in diameter. The match holder which came with your furnace is for the purpose of going down through that hole with a lighted match to the burner down below. Just repeat the same steps that I went through here with the hot water heater. If you get confused because things look a little different, read the instruction plate. Don't panic, don't give up too easily. I've relighted hundreds of pilots, and I still sometimes have to stop and read those instruction plates again. Unless you do this every day, you quickly forget."

OIL FURNACES

I wondered about something. "How about oil furnaces? They don't have pilots."

"They have the same basic problem, they go off and they stay off because they have the same built-in safety feature. It's a box-like device which sticks out of the furnace flue pipe. This box houses the stack control relay system. A heat sensor sticks into the flue pipe. When the furnace cycles on, if in 30 seconds no heat comes up the stack, the sensor will send a command to turn off the burner. Everything stops dead. If it didn't, the gun type oil burner would just keep pumping and spraying oil into the firebox until the storage tank was empty.

"There is a red button on that relay box that you press to re-set the relay and get back into operation again. The furnace will cycle on again, but it will run 30 seconds and stop again unless the oil is ignited and heat comes up that stack. So the big question is, why did the oil fail to ignite in the first place? It could be, and usually is, because the electrodes are getting hit by the oil spray. This should not be and happens only when the spray nozzles are dirty. This deflects and oil spray so that it hits the electrodes. No spark jumps across that ¼-inch electrode gap and the oil is not ignited.

"The nozzles can be cleaned, but a better solution is to just replace them because they aren't much bigger then your thumb and don't cost much. You can buy them at Sears or from any heating contractor. But you must replace with the same spray angle. Stamped on the nozzle is a figure like 45°, 50°, 55°. This is the angle of spray coming out of the nozzle. The electrodes are positioned just on the edge of that spray, but not in it. The wrong nozzle will put the electrodes either too far away or in the oil spray. Of course, the electrodes can be re-positioned, but this is tricky. It's so much easier to just get the right nozzle. So take the old one with you."

Replacing Oil Burner Nozzles

"On top of the burner is a small box. This is the transformer which supplies the 5,000 volts which arcs across those electrodes to ignite the oil. You loosen one finger nut and the box swings up and away on a hinge. There underneath will be exposed the nozzle-electrode assembly unit. It will be hooked into a ¼-inch oil line with a flared coupling. Loosen this flared fitting with a wrench and the whole assembly lifts up and comes out easily. You can now see the nozzle right on the end, with the electrodes positioned on each side. It comes off easily with two wrenches."

I always feel embarrassed and a little stupid when somebody shows me how to do something, and then I find out later that simple instructions were right there under my nose. Everything that Charley told me about relighting the pilots was on a instruction plate attached to both the hot water heater and furnace. Even Wanda could have easily re-lit the pilot if she had read those instructions.

But as Charley said, "Nobody *ever* reads the instruction plate. They just panic. Then they pay some kid in a van with a rusty old machinist's vice hanging on the back 20 or 40 bucks to relight their furnace pilot light. Then they moan and cry about how much everything costs.

I was still suffering from a deflated ego when our garbage disposal conked out. It didn't groan, hum or anything. It just died with nothing in it but two banana skins and some dry bread. I looked for a circuit breaker button, but could find none. So again I went to good old Charley.

"Yeah, I know," he said, "there's a red button on there all right, but they put it in a difficult place to reach. The bottom of your disposal almost touches a shelf. The button is on the bottom and if you've got skinny hands you just might be able to squeeze in there. You know, it's too bad."

"What is?"

"Manufacturers equip their homes with only name brand appliances, like refrigerators, dishwashers, cooking ranges, and automatic washers. But when it comes to garbage disposals, they buy some Mickey Mouse toy that strains and groans running down mashed potatoes. Whenever one of these cheap pieces of junk goes dead, it's because it jammed on a pork chop bone or something. Jamming causes an overload on that little ¼-horse motor, which kicks out the circuit breaker. With a ½-horse motor they wouldn't jam."

GARBAGE DISPOSALS

"If it's jammed, what do I do?" I asked.

"Get a stick and un-jam it. Get that turntable down there moving. When it does, then you reset the circuit breaker. If your hands are too fat, ask the wife to reach under there. Just tell her to feel around until something gives. That'll be the button. Now turn on the cold water and switch on the disposal. It should run. If it doesn't and you hear a hum instead, shine a flashlight down into the grinding chamber and watch what happens when you flip the switch on and off. If the turntable starts to move slightly, then stops with a hum, you have starter winding problems. Check again to be sure. Switch it on, then give the turntable a nudge with your stick. It will start to run. Try again without nudging with the stick. If it won't run, just hums, it's the starter windings. This is a very common problem with some cheap brands of garbage disposal."

"What do I do? It's still in warranty."

"Flush the warranty down the toilet."

"Then how will I get it fixed?"

"Don't."

"Why?"

"Why spend a hundred bucks to fix a lousy $29.95 garbage disposal? Worse yet, if you take the thing out yourself and return it to the manufacturer, they just might send you a new one, and then you'll have to go through this all over again."

"What'll I do then?"

"Junk it, buy a new one and put it in yourself. That's your best move, believe me. Get yourself a ½-horse outfit with an all stainless steel grinding chamber, which is the only kind to get because it stays clean, and never smells or mildews when you're away on vacation. And make sure it's got continuous feed, which will never jam on you."

"What's a continuous feed?"

"That's what you got—that's the only kind they put in mobile homes."

Installing a Garbage Disposal

"Why?" I asked.

"They're the easiest to install. If you decide to buy some other name brand of disposal, stick with continuous feed to simplify your wiring hook-up. If you buy a batch feed type, which does not use a wall switch, the wiring will be different and this might throw you unless you're an electrician, or have some considerable electrical know-how."

"Why is batch feed wired different?"

"Because of the switch. The sink stopper activates a switch when you turn it. The batch feed is more apt to jam because you fill it with garbage first, then turn it on. In continuous feed, garbage is gradually run into the disposal in small amounts. With a ½-horse power and continuous feed, you'll never jam again."

So I did as Charley suggested, bought a ½-horse model for $59.95, and installed it myself with no difficulty, using just the instructions that came with the unit. The old unit first had to be removed (Fig. 4-4) by loosening three bolts at the top. However, before starting this project, it will be so much easier if those two cabinet doors to the area under the sink are removed. Also remove everything from the work area, especially those coffee cans filled with cooking fat. Go the the electrical panel and trip the circuit breaker switch for the kitchen sink area. This will knock out your sink lights, so plug in your trouble light in another room. Double check by switching on the disposal to see if it runs or still hums.

Now disconnect the plumbing as shown in drawing. Unsplice two wires at the cable connection. The unit may have to be turned before it will drop down and come out easily. The sink drain flange will now have to also be removed because each manufacturer has his own type. Usually there will be a large 3½ inch lock nut underneath which you tighten and loosen with a hammer and screwdriver.

Between the flange and the sink there will be two gaskets. One is thick rubber, the other is steel. When you install sink drain, be sure that steel gasket is *between* the lock nut and the rubber gasket, otherwise the locknut will be impossible to draw up tight. Of course, you must seal the sink side of the drain flange with a white caulking compound. Put it on liberally, scrape off the excess, and clean up the mess with lighter fluid.

The new unit will go on much the same as the old one came off. The new wires will splice black-to-black, white-to-white. You ground the unit to a water pipe from any screw that's handy.

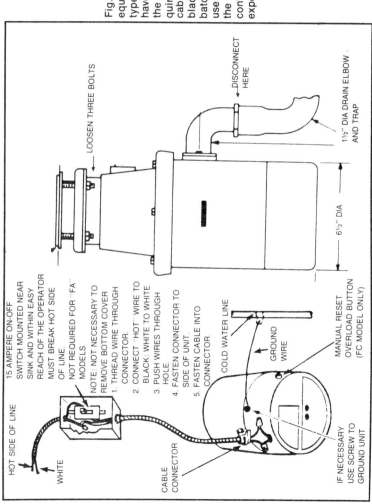

Fig. 4-4. Mobile homes are usually equipped with continuous feed type garbage disposals, which have a wall switch. As seen here, the wiring is very simple and requires only the splicing of the two cable connector wires, black on black and white on white. The batch feed type disposals do not use the wall switch. This means the wiring is different and could confuse you if you lack electrical experience.

LOOSEN THREE BOLTS

DISCONNECT HERE

1½" DIA DRAIN ELBOW AND TRAP

6½" DIA

15 AMPERE ON-OFF SWITCH MOUNTED NEAR SINK AND WITHIN EASY REACH OF THE OPERATOR MUST BREAK HOT SIDE OF LINE.

NOT REQUIRED FOR "FA" MODELS

NOTE: NOT NECESSARY TO REMOVE BOTTOM COVER

1. THREAD WIRE THROUGH CONNECTOR.
2. CONNECT "HOT" WIRE TO BLACK; WHITE TO WHITE.
3. PUSH WIRES THROUGH HOLE.
4. FASTEN CONNECTOR TO SIDE OF UNIT.
5. FASTEN CABLE INTO CONNECTOR.

COLD WATER LINE

GROUND WIRE

MANUAL RESET OVERLOAD BUTTON (FC MODEL ONLY)

HOT SIDE OF LINE

WHITE

CABLE CONNECTOR

IF NECESSARY USE SCREW TO GROUND UNIT

The sewer drain hookup may not be precisely the same as the old one, but it doesn't matter because you have such great flexibility here with those curved traps. You can adjust them to work something out.

Check for leaks before you put the cabinet doors back on. Any leak will be in the drain connection. Make a second check under pressure by completely filling your sink with cold water, then pull out the stopper and turn on the unit. This pressure leak test also flushes out your sewer line and helps to prevent stoppages. If you have a front kitchen with a long sewer line, it's a good idea to pressure flush once every day to keep those coffee grounds moving. If you see no leaks, the job is finished and you can put the cabinet door back on.

Saving Money on Garbage Disposals

When I did this job in my home, I did not splice the electrical connections. I put male and female electric plugs on the wires instead. The reason: I can unplug my garbage disposal and have it out in exactly 15 minutes.

When I bought my garbage disposal, I bought two of them exactly alike. I keep the second unit as a back-up quarterback. If the first unit gives my trouble, out it comes! In goes the back-up unit. The problem disposal goes back to the store and they give me a new one in a box. This can go on forever. I will never, *never* again spend a dime on garbage disposals.

5
Save On
Common Repairs

One of the first things I was asked when friends visited us in our new mobile home was, "How do you keep the pipes from freezing?"

I mumbled something about a "special fiberglass wrapping," then quickly changed the subject.

Frankly, I didn't really know. I had seen pipes around the park heavily wrapped in some kind of aluminum-colored tape, but I wasn't sure what was under all that wrapping. And amazingly, there are others living in mobile homes who are just as ignorant on the subject. Of course, we all know that *something* has been done, but we don't know *what*. We all find out eventually because nothing in life is permanent, and nothing is less permanent than what is done to protect mobile home plumbing in cold weather sections of the country.

One of my neighbors, Sherman K., is a scholarly electrical engineer who works on big contract jobs like nuclear power plants. Sherman awes me for many reasons, but mainly because he buys a new Mark IV every year, the plush $15,000 model. He gets a lot of respect.

WHY THE PIPES DON'T FREEZE

When I asked Sherman about the pipes, he said, "They are protected from freezing by a patented device called a *heat tape* (Fig. 5-1). This is a low resistance wire encased in a flat rubber cover about an inch wide. It is then wrapped around water pipes. It can be covered with insulation, or even left uncovered. Do you understand the theory of electrical resistance?"

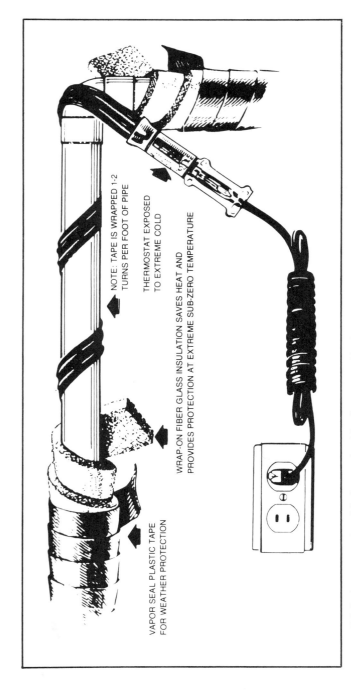

VAPOR SEAL PLASTIC TAPE
FOR WEATHER PROTECTION

WRAP-ON FIBER GLASS INSULATION SAVES HEAT AND
PROVIDES PROTECTION AT EXTREME SUB-ZERO TEMPERATURE

THERMOSTAT EXPOSED
TO EXTREME COLD

NOTE: TAPE IS WRAPPED 1-2
TURNS PER FOOT OF PIPE

Fig. 5-1. This is the way most mobile home plumbing is protected in the severe winter north sections of the country. This is an automatic type electric heat tape with both a thermostat and, right ahead of it, a pilot light. The problem with this type of installation is that the thermostat always ends up under the home where it is often considerably warmer than outside.

"I don't even understand electricity," I said. "What is it?"

"In a nutshell, electrons in motion. If you can make an electron move, you will create energy—the energy we call electricity. If you interfere with the movement of this energy, you create resistance. When electricity fights to overcome this resistance, it consumes energy, which is dissipated as heat. That is the principle behind all heating devices like toasters, steam irons, cooking ranges, and home heating systems. That red-hot wire you see in your toaster is electricity overcoming high resistance. The more the resistance, the more energy is consumed, the more heat is dissipated, the more kilowatt hours of usage are recorded on your electric meter. In other words, high resistance costs money, as any homeowner with electric heat will confirm.

"The resistance in heat tapes is low, about 5 watts per foot. However, some tapes can be quite long, and the wattage adds up. The average length in most mobile home installations will be about 20 feet, which adds up to 100 watts."

Cost of Operating Heat Tapes

"Hey," I interrupted. "Can't that make the old electric bill climb?"

"Yes and no. The 100-watt tape consumes a kilowatt hour of energy every 10 hours, which will cost about 4 cents. Do you know what a kilowatt hour is?"

"No," I said.

"Kilo is from the Greek, and means thousand. Kilowatt is a thousand watts. A kilowatt hour, or KWH, is a 100-watt light bulb burning for 10 hours, or it can also be ten 100-watt bulbs burning for only 1 hour. It all amounts to the same thing. A KWH of energy consumed at the average going residential rate of roughly 4 cents per KWH. In a 30-day period the tape will be on for 720 hours. Multiply this by 100-watts and you get 72,000 watts, or 72 KWH. Multiply 72 by 4 cents and you get $2.88, the cost of operating that 20-foot tape for one month.

"The above cost, however, applies only to the non-automatic types of heat tapes, which are on constantly regardless of outside temperatures. There are automatic heat tapes that have built-in thermostats, both with and without a pilot light which signals when the heat tape is on. The automatics usually switch on at outside temperatures of 36° or 38°, and go off at about 40°.

"With the non-automatic tapes, you can buy a separate thermostat, even fancy deluxe models. With the deluxe models you can set your own on and off temperatures. I have one of these in my home, with an extra pilot light mounted outside my bathroom window where I can easily see it without going outside or looking under the house. It is important to constantly monitor that heat tape.

"If you like to travel first class and want to make a permanent heat tape installation, the Smith-Gates Corporation makes a super deluxe model with a super deluxe price. There is no rubber in this tape to deteriorate. It's round instead of flat and is made of fine mesh copper braid. It will last forever, they say."

Why Pipes Sometimes Freeze

"The standard flat rubber tapes, which is what all set-up crews use, do a good job if properly installed, but even then they have to be replaced even though the manufacturers claim they are guaranteed for a lifetime. They're reasonably safe in making such a claim because 'lifetime' is a relative thing. Auto batteries are guaranteed for 'the life of your car.' How much 'life' is there left in a 10-year-old car? How much 'lifetime' is there left for a retired couple living in a mobile home?

"Play it safe and figure two years as the average life expectancy of the cheaper rubber-covered heat tapes. You might get by three, four, or five years. I know one that is still functioning in the freezing winds off Lake Erie after 10 years. I know of three that went bad the second winter in just this park alone. It probably isn't fair to say they went bad because other factors could have been involved in the pipe freeze-ups, like a bad installation."

"What is a bad installation?" I asked.

"For one, leaving the tape end lie on the ground at the bottom of the water riser. I'm talking about that three-foot hole in the ground encased in a column of drainage tile. That's where your water pipe and shut-off valve emerges from the ground. The top of the tile is usually covered with a wood lid, but this does not keep out water.

"The usual starting point for winding a heat tape is at the bottom of the riser hole near the shut-off valve. If the small plastic knob at the end of the heat tape is left lying on the ground, and water gets in the riser hole, it will eventually short out the tape by seeping through that knob. That plastic knob is the weak link in your heat tape. Mobile home service people have told me it is the major cause of tape failures and water freeze-ups.

HOW TO INSTALL HEAT TAPE

"When you install new tape, start winding it on three feet from the end, and leave that end loose until you finish. Then you come back and tie up that loose end *off the bottom*. Although heat tapes are encased in rubber and are capable of operating in water, they deteriorate fast and won't last more than six months. This is the main reason for first year tape failures and freeze-ups. Although the park is responsible for maintenance of the water riser, they will not pump out the water. Remember now, that is *your* problem."

Protecting the Water Riser

"Most water risers are under the home where they are protected from the weather. But some are off the side, out in the open. If on the driveway side, the carport will protect them. If there is no carport, then the riser must be covered by something better than that wood lid, which is put on there mainly to prevent serious injuries should somebody step in that hole. My riser is protected by my completely enclosed carport, but I still have it covered with brick and tile for safety and esthetic reasons."

Danger of Overlapping Heat Tape

"Another reason for tape failure is overlapping at the end when you finish with a few feet of excess tape and no place to put it. Do *not* go back and over-wind, letting one lap touch another. Even the professionals make this error. Incidentally, the most critical area to be protected is that last one foot of pipe which goes up through the floor into the home. This is where most freeze-ups occur because sometimes they run out of tape when they get here. Also, the thermostat is on this end here and often it will be covered with insulation. The thermostat must be left exposed to the air and to the *coldest* air the pipe will encounter.

Why Separate Thermostat Is Best

"This is the reason I use a separate thermostat hooked into a non-automatic heat tape. With the automatic tapes, your thermostat ends up under the home where the temperature can often be 10 degrees warmer than it is outside around your water riser. When the temperature reaches 36° under the home, it will be 26° at that elbow over your riser—and that is where it freezes. My thermostat is the adjustable-temperature type which I installed on an outside wall of my home. Sure, it costs more, but the peace of mind is worth every cent. If you ever have to crawl around under your home in sub-zero weather replacing burst pipe and installing new tape, you'll understand why."

"Do you have to put anything over the tape?" I asked.

"That depends."

"On what?"

Insulating Over Heat Tape

"On where you live. There are tables available which tell you exactly what protection you can expect at various options (Fig. 5-2). You must take into consideration the wind chill factor with pipe that is out in the open and not protected by skirting. For example, at zero temperature and 20 mph winds, you have a chill factor of 40 below. At 40 degrees, with the same wind velocity, you would have a chill factor of 18 degrees. This is the reason why those windshield washing solutions that you use in your car will sometimes freeze when they hit the glass as you drive, even though they are protected from freezing to about 30 below. If the outside temperature is 10 degrees and you're driving 40 miles an hour, the chill factor on your windshield is 36 below."

This conversation with my electrical engineer neighbor got me to worrying. I had never thought about wind and chill factors. Nobody ever does, until it's too late. I spoke to Charley about it and he said, "Stop worrying. If you ever have a freeze-up, it will only be in that short length of pipe going up through the floor. Sometimes the boys leave a few inches uncovered there."

"Suppose it freezes," I said.

"First you have to be sure."

"How do I find out?"

WHAT TO DO IN A FREEZE-UP

"You check the pilot light to see if your tape is functioning. If it is, the freeze-up is not general. It's in a piece of uncovered pipe somewhere, like I said, right at the end where the boys ran out of tape. So they cover the bare pipe with fiberglass insulation so the boss won't notice. The freeze-up here is easy to break, you can almost do it by just holding your hands over the pipe. A propane torch will have it open in a second.

"However, if the pilot light is not burning, then you better move fast because you have a general freeze-up, and that can mean busted pipes if you don't hurry."

"Hurry for what?" I said.

To select correct heater you must know pipe size, pipe length and lowest temperature expected. From table determine heater needed per foot of pipe and multiply times pipe length to find heater length required. Use ONLY closest standard length. Thermostatic control MUST be used when insulating.

PROTECTION GUIDE—HEATER TAPE APPLIED TO BARE METAL PIPE

NOMINAL PIPE SIZE	TAPE APPLIED STRAIGHT ON PIPE		TAPE APPLIED 3 TURNS PER FOOT OF PIPE		TAPE APPLIED 6 TURNS PER FOOT OF PIPE	
	PROTECTED TO °F	LENGTH OF TAPE REQUIRED PER FT. OF PIPE	PROTECTED TO °F	LENGTH OF TAPE REQUIRED PER FT. OF PIPE	PROTECTED TO °F	LENGTH OF TAPE REQUIRED PER FT. OF PIPE
3/8	−26	1'	−34	1' 2"	−53	1' 6"
1/2	−15	1'	−24	1' 3"	−45	1' 6"
3/4	−5	1'	−16	1' 4"	−40	1' 11"
1	+2	1'	−11	1' 6"	−36	2' 4"
1¼	+8	1'	−7	1' 8"	−34	2' 10"
1½	+11	1'	−5	1' 10"	−33	3' 2"
2	+16	1'	−3	2' 2"	−32	3' 11"
3	+21	1'	−1	3' 0"	−31	5' 7"
4	+23	1'	0	3' 8"	−30	7' 2"
6	+26	1'	+1	5' 4"	−30	10' 6"

PROTECTION GUIDE—WITH ADDITION OF ½" FIBERGLASS INSULATION & OUTER WRAP

NOMINAL PIPE SIZE	TAPE APPLIED STRAIGHT ON PIPE		TAPE APPLIED 3 TURNS PER FOOT OF PIPE		TAPE APPLIED 6 TURNS PER FOOT OF PIPE	
	PROTECTED TO °F	LENGTH OF TAPE REQUIRED PER FT. OF PIPE	PROTECTED TO °F	LENGTH OF TAPE REQUIRED PER FT. OF PIPE	PROTECTED TO °F	LENGTH OF TAPE REQUIRED PER FT. OF PIPE
⅜	−45	1'	−55	1' 2"	−78	1' 6"
½	−30	1'	−43	1' 3"	−68	1' 6"
¾	−18	1'	−32	1' 4"	−64	1' 11"
1	−8	1'	−25	1' 6"	−59	2' 4"
1¼	0	1'	−20	1' 8"	−56	2' 10"
1½	+4	1'	−17	1' 10"	−55	3' 2"
2	+10	1'	−15	2' 2"	−53	3' 11"
3	+17	1'	−12	3' 0"	−51	5' 7"
4	+20	1'	−11	3' 8"	−51	7' 2"
6	+24	1'	−10	5' 4"	−50	10' 6"

Fig. 5-2.   This heat tape chart will help you determine how much tape you need to buy and what protection you can expect with and without insulation. Only you can decide how much protection you need.

"To get the water moving before it freezes solid! Open all your faucets, cut the old insulation and tape off as quickly as possible, then go over the pipe with a propane torch until you get some water movement. The important thing at this point is to get the water moving, to prevent a solid freeze which will crack the pipe. So long as the water is moving, even a trickle, you've bought yourself time in which to drive to the store for a new heat tape and insulation material. Keep the faucets open while you're working."

Emergency Freeze-Up Repair Kits

"A fishing friend of mine over on Catawba Island keeps an emergency repair kit on hand for just such occasions. It consists of a propane torch, with spare cylinders, a spare heat tape and insulation materials, some copper tubing in various lengths, flaring tools and a good supply of flared couplings, unions and elbows. If he has a burst water pipe, the bad section is cut out and he flares in a new piece of pipe in just a few minutes.

"I have those same emergency supplies on hand in my workshop, but not for myself. It's for people in the park who call good old Charley when they can't get anybody else on Sunday."

"How come you don't need those emergency supplies?" I asked.

A Better Protection System

"Because I have a better protection system for myself," he said. "When I replaced my heat tape recently, I went a step further. I wound *two* heat tapes on my water pipe. But only one tape is plugged in. That second tape is the back-up quarterback ready to take over in a second. If I have a freeze-up, it only takes a second to unplug the bad tape and plug in the good one and I'm thawed out in minutes with no fuss or bother."

A wonderful idea. I thanked Charley for giving it to me, and to you.

HEAT TAPES ON SEWER LINES

Can heat tapes be used on sewer lines? I wondered about this, and investigated. I was told, "yes and no." Some mobile home manufacturers still use iron sewer pipe. On them heat tape could be used. But most home manufacturers have switched to plastic pipe. One maker of heat tapes warns *not* to use them on plastic pipe. Yet another maker of heat tapes says his product *can* be used on plastic pipe, if it is of high quality, whatever that means. However, in the instruction sheet, this manufacturer advises that the tape can be used on plastic pipe only if it is not covered by fiberglass insulation. The 5-watts-per-foot, they say, does not produce enough heat to harm plastic pipe unless it is retained with insulation.

Why Sewer Lines Rarely Freeze

When I questioned a general plumbing contractor on this, he said, "You don't really need a heat tape on a sewer line, especially in this part of the country where mobile homes have skirting and shrubbery as protection against high winds. Suspended sewer lines hanging under a home will not freeze, if properly installed, because water is only passing through the pipe for a few seconds. It isn't in there long enough to freeze."

Why Sewer Lines Do Freeze

"However, if the sewer line has a sharp dip in it, and poor drop, waste could settle and build a dam. Water will back up behind that dam. But even this won't sneak up on you overnight. You will have plenty of warning that trouble is coming when your front toilet or kitchen sink starts to back and drain slowly. You will also hear a funny noise, like 'glug, glug.' This means that a stoppage is building up."

Standby Protection

If you live in an area of severe winters and high winds, and you anticipate freeze problems with your sewer line, wrap it with heat tape, but don't turn it on until needed. Just have it there, available on a standby basis with an easily accessible switch on the outside that you can turn on during a sub-zero cold spell and high winds. When the weather moderates, you can switch it off. Even if you never use it, you will have peace of mind.

IN-THE-HOME WATER PROBLEMS

Larry and Jean, new young marrieds who just moved into a new Delta, are already the most popular young couple in my park. This puzzled me at first because mobile home communities are not the most friendly places in the world and newcomers sometimes find it hard to make friends. Not Larry and Jean. They were instant friends with everybody. Then I found out why. A Sears service truck parked in front of Larry's home every day around noon was the reason for their instant acceptance. Larry worked for an appliance discounter as a service technician, making house calls to install and to service television, dryers, refrigerators, and automatic washers.

There were days when Larry almost never left home. All his service calls would be right in the park. When I asked him what he worked on the most, he said, "In mobile home parks, it's the dryers and washers."

I was amazed. "Why washers?"

"They leak."

"Why?"

The Reason Automatic Washers Leak

"Poor installation. Actually it isn't the washer that leaks, it's the hose connections. Those clowns at the factories who hook up the washers don't understand that water at all the hose connections is under pressure. You don't just hand-tighten because they'll leak after a while. That's why all manufacturers recommend you turn off the water when finished, never leave it on permanently. I always have to replace the washers in the hose connections, and tighten them with pliers."

"That the only leak?"

He shook his head sadly. "If a washer is in that bathroom closet, and the floor keeps getting wet, it's that black drain hose with the U-turn on the end which is supposed to hang into a standpipe. In a conventional home installation, that standpipe will be about 4-feet high. In mobile home bathroom installations, the standpipe is under wash basin compartments and is rarely over 18-inches high. When the washer switches to drain cycle, that hose quivers and jumps as the water suddenly comes gushing out under pressure. Sometimes the hose will jump up almost out of that standpipe and water will splash out. This is a very common problem with bathroom washer-dryer installations because of that short standpipe and because the drain hose is just loosely stuck in there with nothing to hold it down. I tell everybody here to tie that hose down with something, improvise some kind of a clamp with hanger strap material—anything to keep it from jumping up."

Clothes Dryer Lint

"What's the problem with dryers?" I asked.

"I hear complaints that furnace filters plug up with lint and I know immediately what it is. In those bathroom type installations, the dryer is stacked on top of the washer, pushed back into a small closet. These are pretty tight quarters and it takes a midget to get behind the dryer to hook up that flexible 4-inch exhaust ducting, which either goes up through the ceiling or down through the floor into the crawl space. So, very frequently, if the factory doesn't employ a midget, that exhaust ducting will not be hooked up to the dryer. The homeowner can see the duct back there running up to his ceiling, or hanging down into his crawl space, so he naturally assumes that the other end is hooked up to his dryer. One of the things that I am learning about mobile homes is that you must never assume *anything*."

"How do you get back there to fix it?" I asked.

Servicing The Dryer

"You don't. You've got to pull the dryer out. It's not heavy, it's just awkward to handle. If you have a utility table, the type with wheels, you can do the job alone by sliding the dryer onto the table, then rolling it out of the way. You've got to get the dryer out of there so you can clean up the mess. Lint will be over everything, and an inch thick on the floor. In one home I serviced recently, the dryer was getting no electricity. When I pulled it out, I found out the exhaust duct was not hooked up. Lint had gotten into the pig-tail electric wall outlet and broken the connection. The entire closet had to be vacuumed. The pig-tail outlet was cleared with a crevice tool. Don't ever stick anything in there until you throw the main switch. The dryer itself was also clogged with lint, and had to be thoroughly vacuumed.

"In every mobile home dryer I worked on, there was enough excess length to the ducting hose that you could easily attach it to the dryer *before* you slide it back in on top of the washer. That's the only way it can be done. Once the dryer's back in that closet, it's impossible to hook up that duct. That's why it never gets done at the factory."

Something bothered me. "When the dryer vents up through the ceiling, where do the heat and lint go?" I asked.

"Into the roof space."

I was aghast. The roof crown is only six inches. I wondered about all that warm air condensing up there between the roof and ceiling.

When I spoke to Charley about this later, he said, "That small space is well ventilated with three air caps on the roof, one on each end, one in the middle. The lint and warm air are quickly exhausted because that space is so small. The crown is six inches, but most of the space is filled with insulation and vapor barrier."

FLOOR MOVEMENT AND SQUEAKING

At a regular monthly meeting of homeowners in a Pontiac, Michigan mobile home park, most of the discussions were devoted to floors that moved and squeaked when you walked over them. They listened to an expert, a building inspector from Detroit, explain that the movement of the floors was due to the lack of support under the homes. Some of the hollow building blocks had settled in the ground more than others, he said, leaving the I-beam frame without support in some column areas. If this occurred in the front or back ends of the home, sudden added weight here would cause floor movement and squeaking.

The rest of the meeting was devoted to determining who was responsible for this problem, and who was going to fix it. Some of the homeowners in this park are still arguing about this, and their floors are still squeaking. But Jim and Martha are impatient people who hate community meetings. So they went ahead and fixed it themselves rather than listen to more discussion and resolution passing.

When I asked Jim why he fixed it himself, he said, "I could see no point in further discussions because the park had nothing to do with setting up my home. They just rented me a lot. I had plenty of time to inspect it and find out my cement block supports would be sitting directly on the ground instead of a concrete pad or ribbons. What's the point of trying to fix responsibility? The sales organization has left town, and the mobile home servicing outfit is a two-bit operation that works out of a post office box and telephone answering service."

"How did you fix it?" I asked.

Correcting The Problem

"I put a foundation under my cement blocks."

"What kind of foundation?"

"Big cement footing blocks, 16 × 16 square. They're solid and very heavy, but they're the next best thing to a poured foundation—in fact, they're called footing blocks because they are used as foundations for buildings on farms. When you can't pour concrete, you use footing blocks." (Fig. 5-3)

"How did you get them under the cement blocks?" I asked.

"I bought a 10-ton screw jack."

"Why a screw jack?"

"With a screw jack you have fine fractional movement up or down. A hydraulic jack goes up in half-inch jumps. You only need to raise the I-beam just enough to clear the blocks so you can pull them out. Then you set in the footing block directly on the ground over a layer of sand for leveling purposes. You do this at each support column. When finished, you stretch a string level between the columns to get them all level."

"What's a string level?" I asked.

"It's a little glass tube of liquid that you hang on a string stretched between two points. It's used for leveling things that are many feet apart. You stretch the string crosswise and lengthwise between the supports, with the glass leveling device hanging in the middle. The bubble in the glass will tell you when the columns are the same height—you may have to use pieces of wood for shim material to fill in small gaps between them."

A Good Foundation

"A good foundation is very important if you have a tag, expando or double, because the two sections don't always settle evenly. If the tag settles on the outside edge, it will pull away at the roof. Just a fraction of an inch is enough to break the caulking seal, and then you've got leaks and ugly stains on the ceiling."

I was disgusted. Why should a homeowner have to do all that hard work? I asked the president of a park betterment association in my own area, and he said, "You don't. Let the home settle. Let the roof leak. You can always catch the water in a bucket. You can

Fig. 5-3. Footing blocks next to the ground under the tag are the next best thing to a poured concrete foundation. Never support a tag, expando, or either half of a double on ordinary building blocks touching the ground directly. When the blocks settle into the ground on the outer edge, the tag will pull away at the roof and open up leaks that will ruin your ceilings.

always write letters to your congressman and to Zip Line, asking questions like 'Aren't there some standards for mobile home foundations?' And Zip Line will tell you 'Local housing codes specify no standards for mobile home foundations because they are of a temporary nature, sitting loosely on the surface of the ground. The mobile home buyer can rely only on the integrity of the dealer, the quality of the park, and the intensity of his own investigations.' "

"Sounds kinda familiar," I said. "What you will get for a foundation when you rent a lot in any park is right out there in the open for God and the whole world to see, and nobody is twisting your arm."

"That's right," he said. "But if you still feel, however, that just as a matter of principle you should fight for your rights, whatever they are, and sue somebody, there will be a hundred people in the park who will praise you, and who will cheer you on, but will offer no help with the legal expenses. Then, just as your lawyer is ready to have papers served, you'll read in the paper that the firm who set up your home has filed bankruptcy.

"Who do you sue now? Well, there's Community Developers, Inc., who sold you the home and made all those promises. So, where are they? Like the Bedouin Arabs, they folded their tents in the night and departed for some new oasis in another state.

"Community Developers, who contracts with new parks to get them filled with homes and operational, is primarily a sales organization. They temporarily manage the park until it is 80 percent filled, collecting the rent from some out-of-town office. Then one day Community Developer's sign in front of the park office is suddenly taken down, you get a notice in the mail that the rent will henceforth be collected by the park's own management office, and will you please come in, at your convenience, and sign your new lease. When you do, you find that the rent has been increased another five bucks.

"So now you've wasted all that money on legal expenses, and you still haven't got those footing blocks. But you got respect because you were ready to fight for a principle. But respect won't help you lift those heavy footing blocks and drag them under your home."

"Then what do you suggest?" I said.

"Buy footing blocks. Stay away from lawyers."

WHY GAS POSTLIGHTS BURN POORLY

The first time Wanda saw those ornamental gas postlights, she thought they were picturesque and nostalgic. She thinks differently now, after finding out how hard it was to buy replacement mantels, and how often they had to be replaced. Bugs and small moths easily get into the lamp housing through ventilating holes and loose-fitting glass. During the summer bug season I had to replace about one mantel a week, at 50 cents each. I went through a box of 24 in our first season.

If properly adjusted for air/gas mixture, the three mantels will produce a light output equivalent to a 100 watt bulb. But very few ever burn properly, as you can tell by driving through any park at night. They either have broken mantels or burn poorly with a yellow flame, creating much black soot. At their worst, they produce the light output of three matches.

Most of this is the fault of the installer, who never leaves with the new homeowner the manufacturer's sheet of instructions, which explains how to adjust the proper air/gas mixture for maximum light and clean combustion. The fact that some service people charge 20 dollars to service the light, plus the cost of mantels at a *dollar* each, may be the motivating factor behind their neglect to leave the instructions, which they just throw away with the carton.

Fig. 5-4. Through that hole in the base of the lamp housing on the right you will find both the gas shut-off valve and the fine air/gas mixture adjustment. It is a screw within a screw and requires two screwdrivers, one broad and one narrow. The outer screw shuts off the gas; the inner screw tunes the air mixture.

Adjusting The Gas/Air Mixture

There is a gas shutoff valve and a fine air adjustment screw through that small hole at the base of the lamp housing (Fig. 5-4). This is actually two screws, or a screw inside a screw. The outer shell of this screw has slots to take a broad screwdriver. With the slots up and down at 12 o'clock, the gas is turned on full. At a quarter turn to the right, 3 o'clock, the gas is turned off.

The small inner screw, which takes a very narrow screwdriver, is the fine air adjustment. This adjustment will almost be too small to affect combustion very much. To get a big adjustment, with a dramatic improvement in light quality, remove two glass panes in the lamp housing. At the base of that center pipe (Fig. 5-5), there is a movable outer sleeve which covers large air holes which you can clearly see in the photo. As you slide this sleeve up or down over those holes, you greatly increase or decrease the air flow until the mantel burns at maximum intensity. Then you make a fine air adjustment with the post screw, backing off a little on the air by screwing in, or clockwise.

Protecting the Mantels From Moths

You can affect a considerable savings in mantel replacement if you cover the ventilation louvers on the top inside of the lamp housing with small squares of screen material, securing them with plastic tape. Do the same with the air holes at the bottom of the lamp housing. This will at least keep out the moths, which break mantels. Nothing will ever keep out the other tiny insects which keep piling up on the bottom inches deep, but at least they don't break mantels. Once a year you clean them out with a vacuum.

CONVERTING FROM GAS TO ELECTRICITY

Sooner or later you will give some thought to the idea of converting the gas postlight to electricity, and almost always right after you get a bill from the gas company with the notation: "Includes gas cost adjustments of $.04387 per CCF." One very annoying thing about the gas lights is that they burn 24 hours a day at a monthly cost of about $7.50. A 100-watt incandescent bulb, burning from dusk to dawn, will cost about $1.44, or half that for a 50-watt bulb.

The Cost of Converting

Most mobile home owners quickly cool on the idea of converting when they learn the cost, that is if they have the job done. The

Fig. 5-5. The fine air adjustment rarely is enough to improve light quality. To really make a worthwhile improvement, you must use the coarse adjustment, which is the round sleeve at the bottom of the gas pipe. Note that the sleeve partially covers large round holes. Sliding the sleeve up or down over those holes changes the air volume. This will really make a change in the light output.

going price in 1975 for an incandescent conversion was $225. For 50-watt mercury vapor, it was $325. For 100-watt mercury vapor, $365.

Is Mercury Vapor Worth the Cost?

Why pay all that extra dough for mercury vapor, and is it worth it?

With incandescent you will be replacing the light bulb about every two months. This means dragging a ladder out to the light post six times a year, in all kinds of weather, to change bulbs. The mercury vapor bulbs cost from 8 to 10 dollars, but they last up to 10 years. And they give out twice as much light. For example, a 50-watt mercury will produce the same light output as a 100-watt incandescent for $.72 cents a month, as compared to $1.44 a month for the 100-watt incandescent. Also, in 10 years you will have replaced about 60 incandescent bulbs. When you consider the cost of all those bulb replacements, and the cost of electricity used, over the long pull, mercury vapor is the cheapest installation.

I was scared to tackle the job myself, but Wanda kept goading me so I talked with my electrical engineer neighbor and he gave me wiring diagrams which looked easy. Then I stalled some more because, as I told Wanda, "I hate to dig up our nice sodded lawn to lay that wire."

Then Charley came along and killed that excuse. I wanted to choke him when he said, "You don't have to dig up your lawn. I could lay that wire under your sod, and tomorrow you wouldn't even know it was there."

That forced me into making a cost estimate.

Cost of Do-It-Yourself Conversion

$10.49 for new lamp housing to fit on existing post.

$10.99 for photo electric switch, with service outlet.

$35.00 mercury ballast, 50-watt

$ 7.49 type UF indoor-outdoor cable, 3-wire, 14 gauge, 50 feet.

$ 8.00 mercury vapor bulb, 50-watt.

―――――

$71.97 total cost for 50-watt mercury vapor conversion.

If you decide on an incandescent conversion, you can eliminate the mercury ballast and bulb, which will bring the cost down to $28.97. If you want even more cost cutting, eliminate the new lamp housing and use the one you already have. Now you're down to $18.48. But since you're using the old housing, you must buy a porcelain light socket and all the necessary attachments for securing it to the lamp base.

The photo-electric switch comes already mounted in a 3-inch diameter black cylinder which fits neatly over your existing lamp post. Your lamp housing, in turn, fits directly over the switch. The photo-electric switch is available either with or without the 120-

volt utility outlet on the opposite side. It costs only a few cents more with the outlet but is worth it, especially if you have an electric lawn mower or trimming shearers.

In the drawings (Figs. 5-6, 5-7, 5-8) you have three wiring options. If you want just the incandescent light bulb, which is the simplest and cheapest conversion, you can save still another two dollars because you don't need 3-wire cable. The porcelain socket will have two loose wires, black and white. The 2-wire cable will also have two wires of the same color code. Splicing the wires, black-on-black, white-on-white is utter simplicity.

If you decide you want the utility outlet, then you must use the 3-wire cable. The third wire on this cable will be just bare copper wire.

If you will examine closely any wall electrical outlet in your home, you will note that there are two slots and one round hole. But notice also that one of the two slots is larger. The large slot is negative ground, or neutral ground. It is the white wire in all electrical work. The smaller slot is positive, or the "hot" wire. This is always the black wire. The round hole in the outlet is the grounding connection, which hooks up to that bare copper wire in the 3-wire cable.

This additional ground connection was made mandatory some years ago as a safety factor to protect you from being accidently electrocuted when handling metal-encased power tools. Things are

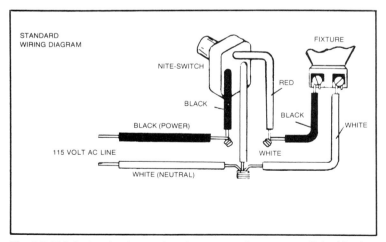

Fig. 5-6. This is the simplest and easiest way to wire your post light. It's also the cheapest because you don't need the more costly two-wires-and-ground cable to hook up an ordinary incandescent light bulb.

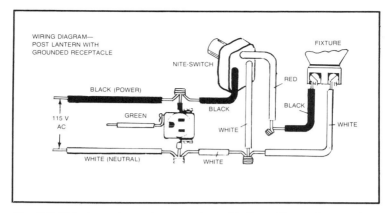

Fig. 5-7. This incandescent conversion with the utility outlet requires three-wire cable (two wires and ground). The extra cost is very small and that extra outlet outside can be very handy, like when you vacuum out your car.

quite compact inside a power tool and sometimes a tiny strand of wire on the hot side may be very close to the metal housing. If you are standing on damp ground, working that tool under heavy load conditions, voltage might seek a path of less resistance and arc across to the metal housing, pass through your body to ground.

A mobile home, since it is all metal, is negative ground. Always remember this when doing any kind of electrical work. A friend of mine didn't, and almost lost his life. He had been standing on a wooden ladder (for safety reasons he said) removing a rusted light fixture on his mobile home. But he forgot about the aluminum siding. Fortunately, he had been holding that light fixture with just one hand when he accidently touched the siding. He got a jolt. Had his other hand been touching the siding, current would have passed through his body and killed him. That's why that third wire, that round hole in all wall sockets is so important in a mobile home. That's why you have to be so careful when you wire those plugs. The screws on the white plated side are neutral ground, the white wire. The screws on the brass side are the "hot" side, the black wire. That screw off by itself on the end, usually painted green, is the round hole wire, which grounds all tools and appliances so you don't get electrocuted.

Performing the Conversion

You are now ready to bring electricity to the postlight. But first you turn off the gas at the meter. The gas light has its own shutoff, a type of valve which requires a wrench. You can't miss it because a small diameter pipe runs directly down to the ground where plastic tubing is coupled to it, then worked all the way back to the light. You do *not* remove this tubing. Just turn off the gas at the meter.

At the base of your lamp post, lay a string line to the point of your skirting where you will enter with the electric wire cable. This marks the line where the wire will be buried, but you do *not* dig up the lawn. You do it Charley's way. With a sharp bread knife you cut a deep incision in the sod along that string line. Then you spread wide the incision to the base of the post. Here you may have to dig and remove some soil to find where the gas line enters the post through a ¾-inch hole. When you find the tubing, cut it. Now remove the lamp housing—just three taping screws hold it—and pull out the gas line as you do. If you bought a new lamp housing, you have no further need for the old one. Give it to a neighbor for spare parts. The four pieces of glass will not fit in your new housing.

Through that same hole at the bottom of the post you work in the stiff wire cable. An easier way to do this is to take a length of aluminum clothesline wire you had left over from your sewer line work (I told you it had many uses) and push it down from the top

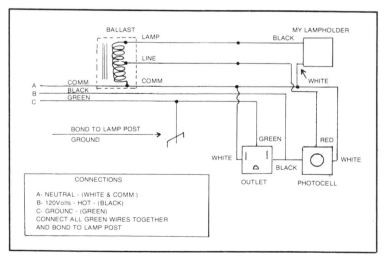

Fig. 5-8. Don't let this mercury vapor wiring diagram frighten you—it's easier than it looks. Just take each wire in turn, and use twist-on wire connectors (not solder) so that if you make a mistake, you can just untwist and start over.

until it reaches that hole, where you can reach it with long-nosed pliers. By putting a U-loop in both wires, you can hook them together, then you pull the gable wire gently up through the post. Leave yourself at least a 12-inch working length at the top. The excess you can stuff back down the post later.

You are now ready to lay the cable wire down into the sod incision, the thin side of this flat wire facing up. Push it down as far as it will go with your finger or a piece of thin wood. Work the wire under the skirting channels into the crawl space. Close the sod incision, and tamp it down by foot. After a watering, you'll never know where it was cut.

Now comes the hard part, crawling on your belly with the loose wire back to that electric outlet box where you plug in the heat tape. This wire need not be covered or secured to anything. It can just lie on the ground. If you attached a three-pronged male plug to the end of this wire, don't plug it in yet. Remember, you still have wire connections to make at the other end.

Use one of the three wiring diagrams which applies to your installation. Plug in under the home, and you're ready for a test. Hold your hand over the photo-electric eye until it activates the switch, and the light should come on. Take your hand off the eye and the light should go off. Incidentally, mercury vapor lights do not come on instantaneously, but go through a slow warm-up before they reach full intensity in about two or three minutes. And that humming sound you hear in your post is the ballast, and is normal.

Now wasn't that easy?

Save On Driveway And Roof Problems

6

Stanley, a maintenance foreman with the state highway department, lives in my park and I follow him around every day as we make 15 laps on our 10-speed. That's how I met Stanley. Not too many people own an imported French racing bike, status symbol of the 10-speed bike snobs. Anybody who does becomes the target of all the professional bike thieves. We got to talking one day about how we protected our bikes from theft.

For two days I missed Stanley. Knowing how religious he was about physical fitness, I stopped off at his home on East Daisy Lane for a check. He had just finished blacktopping his driveway and I was appalled. It was a very hot July day and I said, "You crazy, man? You could have a heat stroke."

He shrugged. "You gotta do this on a very hot day."

"Why?"

"It spreads easy, dries fast."

"I mean, why do you have to *do* it?"

"Why do you have to wash and wax you car every Sunday?"

"It looks better."

"And that makes you feel better."

"Is that the only reason for all this hard work on a hot day—it makes you *feel* better? I wouldn't do it."

"You will," he said.

"How do you know?"

"I did it. Everybody in the park who matters did it. And you will too because you don't want to lose class."

WHY BLACKTOP A DRIVEWAY?

"Is that the only reason for putting that stuff on? Now I know why management doesn't blacktop the streets here in the park and why you don't blacktop state roads."

"Wait a minute now," he said. "I didn't risk cardiac failure in this hot sun just to maintain my social standing. I never do anything without a reason, and there *is* a reason for doing this."

"That's what I wanna know," I said. "This is a stinking and messy job. I don't want to do it without a good reason."

"First, a driveway does look better after it's been coated. Second, it's better conditioned to live with two automobiles."

"Why?"

"They constantly drip oil. They drip salt in the winter. Bituminous driveways are a mixture of sand and small stones with an asphalt binder which holds it all together in a cohesive glob. If the surface of this glob is not protected with a waterproof coating of some kind, tiny cracks and fissures will form to permit water and car drippings to enter. In winter, the water which seeps in freezes and damages the asphalt binder. This causes the stone and sand to loosen and wash away. Then you have an ugly hole. The kind that shakes you up when you hit it unexpectedly on a rainy night and it's filled with water.

"Another thing, the asphalt binder is a petroleum derivative. That means it is soluable in all petroleum distillates. The drippings from your car acts as a solvent to soften the asphalt binder so that when you drive over it, your tires leave a deep tread mark. In time, this also will become a hole."

"How did you learn all this?" I said.

"The state of Ohio spends millions every year on road maintenance. Some of that money goes for research. I get new data and research reports every week from Columbus, like one about the effects of frost and sunlight on state secondary roads, which are mostly asphalt surfaces. The actinic rays of the sun oxidize the bitumen. Acting together, frost and sunlight reduce adhesion which binds the mixture together. With adhesion gone, the glob disintegrates in an uneven manner. You'll have stretches of good surface, then you'll hit a bad stretch all broken up like peanut brittle. The trucking industry has been getting some blame for this, but it really isn't their fault.

"This stuff that I put on my driveway today is still in the testing stage. I got a sample from the manufacturer. But I don't think it's much different from any of the new products they're coming out with today. All the better driveway sealers are made up of specially formulated coal tar pitch emulsions, and they all have some new patented additive which is supposed to protect bituminous driveways against oxidation and brittleness caused by the sun and weather. Nobody yet has come up with total protection. All you get is a delaying action, a resistance to the softening action of drippings from your car, and a temporary waterproofing of the surface to prevent entrance of water."

"Why don't the state and county use that new stuff?" I asked. "Wouldn't that reduce maintenance costs?"

The New Sealers

"Yes and no. First, the new products are expensive. Over the long pull, it's far cheaper for us to just fill the holes, and we get less complaints."

"What do you mean?"

"Have you ever bought a new car and then been forced to drive over a section of road that had just been sprayed with a blacktop coating? Remember how mad you were? Your brand new car was a mess, tar all over the wheelcovers and white sidewalls. Remember that nasty letter you wrote to your state senator in Columbus? Well, that is one of the main reasons why we have stopped blacktopping secondary roads plus the cost factor. With a few dumptruck loads of of bituminous mixture, we can patch up all the state roads in a few weeks, with no complaints from the taxpayers. But to blacktop *all* the secondary state roads would cost millions, and a million notes to the administration in an angry backlash from motorists whose cars were messed up by tar."

"What's the park's excuse for not blacktopping?" I asked.

Why The Park Doesn't Blacktop

"Same as the state and the county. Tenants in the park would howl if they couldn't use the streets for a few days. Mothers would also howl when children and pets picked up tar and tracked it into the house and on those beautiful pile rugs. It's quite a problem and not as simple as you or I blacktopping an enclosed driveway over which we have complete control. Park management has enough trouble with tenants and they're just not looking for new problems. So the streets are not blacktopped, and probably never will be."

WHY ROOFS ARE COATED

I pointed across the street to another mobile homer, stripped bare to the waist in the hot sun, painting his roof. I said, "Now why is *that* necessary? The roof is galvanized iron. It won't rust."

"Oh yes it will. Wherever galvanized iron is sharply bent or cut it will rust. And bare metal absorbs heat. You can fry eggs on a mobile home roof."

"What's he putting on the roof?"

"A special coating to eliminate roof rumble."

"Roof *what?*"

"Rumble. You mean you haven't heard it yet?"

"Am I supposed to?"

"Only when the wind blows."

"Good Grief! Anything *else?*"

He smiled. "Mobile home roofs have problems which are exclusively mobile home problems. In fact, a dozen new companies have come into existence recently, and they all make special new products for mobile home roofs."

"What causes roof rumble?" I asked.

"Wind and rain. The air space under a mobile home roof is very small, at most less than six inches in the center, less than nothing at the sides. High winds cause rapid changes of air pressure under the roof. This makes the metal buckle with a booming rumble. It can be very annoying at night when you're trying to sleep. You lay there waiting for the next rumble. It's like waiting for a shoe to drop. A company in Cleveland has developed a new product to correct this. It's called 'Quiet Roof'. You spread it on with a roof brush at a rate of about a gallon per 20 sq. ft. That's pretty doggone heavy for an area only 5 by 4 feet."

"It must go on a half inch thick," I gasped (Fig. 6-1).

"It would have to," he said, "to be effective. It cures without hardening, and completely stops roof rumble. It also provides a weather-proofing, leak-sealing, sun-reflecting roof coating. A single wide 70 × 12 would take about 42 gallons of the stuff."

"The sheer weight of all that paint should cure *anything,*" I said.

"It's better than laying patio blocks on the roof like some homeowners do. You get a hundred cement patio blocks on a roof, and then four inches of wet snow on top of that, and you might find the whole mess in bed with you. Mobile home roofs are structured to handle big snow loads, but not snow *and* cement blocks."

"Does your roof rumble?" I asked.

"Not yet. But if it ever does, I'll use the paint. It's not cheap, but if it does the job, what the hell. I might even use it anyway, just as insurance against leaks. That's another mobile home failing— leaks that develop after heavy snows."

Fig. 6-1. "Quiet Roof" must go on thick to be effective. A gallon covers no more than twenty square feet. You just use the brush to move it around, like spreading butter on toast.

LEAKS AFTER SNOW

"Why after a snow?"

"Six inches of wet snow is a tremendous weight. You weren't here last winter to see all the carports caving in under the snow. That massive weight on a home roof causes movement around ventilators and chimneys. This breaks the caulking seals of ordinary cement, which gets hard and has no elasticity. This 'Quiet Roof' stuff never gets hard and will stretch and give without cracking to open up a leak."

After this conversation with Stanley, I made a thorough investigation of 'Quiet Roof' and other products because I have a pathological fear of leaks, something I acquired as a Lake Erie yachtsman. I used to spend half the boating season tracking down those mysterious leaks which every boat has and which everybody else just ignores. I would be sleeping in my bunk, a drop of water would hit me in the eye, and I would spend the rest of the night looking for the leak.

EMERGENCY LEAK REPAIRS

The Cleveland firm which manufactures "Quiet Roof" has another special item which they call "Emergency Aluminum Patch-

Fig. 6-2. "Emergency Aluminum Patching Cement," another Kool Seal product, can be applied even while it is raining and on wet surfaces. You should have a supply of this on hand, ready when needed. You can be as certain as death and taxes that it will be needed.

ing Cement." The remarkable thing about this stuff is that you can brush it right over a wet surface to instantly plug leaks (Fig. 6-2). As the old joke goes, the roof only leaks when it rains. And that is precisely when you can't do a thing about the leak with most other products because the instructions on the label will say "Use only on dry surfaces." This product can also be used to instantly plug leaks, and fill big voids around flashings, stacks, seams, and chimneys right in the middle of a rain storm.

Another chronic leak problem is that long seam where the tag and main home come together. I found many temporary solutions to this, but for a permanent job it takes more than ordinary black roof cement. The Electric Paint & Varnish Co. of Cleveland, which makes "Quiet Roof," has a special adhesive which you spread over the seam, then lay a membrane material over the adhesive and roll it down (Fig. 6-3). When this dries to touch, you brush it down with aluminum roof coating (Fig. 6-4). Anything less than this is only a temporary correction of this very persistent leak because mobile homes are all metal, and metal is constantly expanding and contracting every single day.

New Leak Stoppers

Two other new products which do the same thing as the membrane material, but in a different way, are "Miracle Seal" and "Flex-O-Patch." Both of these are self-sticking synthetic rubber which come in 25 foot rolls, 2½ and 8 inches wide, backed with a

130

Fig. 6-3. This is the only way you will ever permanently stop that roof leak where the tag and home join. This membrane method is by Kool Seal, but Miracle Seal's synthetic rubber tape in the 8-inch size will also do the job. You can forget about conventional caulking methods.

specially treated paper to prevent sticking. You cut off what you need, press it against the surface (Fig. 6-5), then peel away the paper. It will mold and stick to any surface (Fig. 6-6, 6-7) and remains permanently flexible under all weather conditions from

Fig. 6-4. After the Kool Seal membrane is set into the adhesive, it must be painted over in this manner with a fibrated coating (aluminum or white) or Quiet Roof.

Fig. 6-5. Miracle Seal is easy to use. You just cut the length that you need, press the rubber tape down over the seam or leaking area, which it will immediately adhere to, then peel away the paper backing.

65° below to 180° above zero. They will not shrink, harden, crack, become brittle or oxidize.

These are the only products available today that have the necessary elasticity for that difficult carport-to-home seam which is impossible to leak-proof with anything else. Covering this synthetic rubber with aluminum roof coating, after application, will give it additional protection from the sun. It will last indefinitely. If one of these two products were used at the time awnings, carports, and gutters were installed, they would virtually eliminate all future caulking.

Conventional caulking materials that stop leaks on wood homes are almost useless on mobile homes. Commercial awning-carport companies will make an installation on Monday and by Saturday there are dirt streaks down the side of the home caused by leaking.

Conventional Caulking Materials

Commercial installers use conventional caulking materials in the conventional way—a caulking gun, which is fast and convenient for *them*. That's the way they have always done it on wood homes. So that's the way they do it on mobile homes. But it just won't work on metal-to-metal surfaces which are subject to extreme temperature changes. In Florida, California, New Mexico, and Arizona you

132

Fig. 6-6. Miracle Seal will mold easily to fit any shape, and will stick to anything.

can fry pancakes on mobile home roofs. Yet at night those same metal surfaces will be ice cold. And that is the main reason for coating a mobile home roof.

Fibrous and Non-Fibrous Coatings

Most roof coatings have mixed in with the paint a fibrous material which acts as an insulating barrier between the sun and the

Fig. 6-7. Miracle Seal's flexibility and adhesion are demonstrated here.

metal. This binder is non-hardening and remains permanently flexible. Aluminum pigmentation, also mixed with the binder, is for reflective purposes. In southern climates, where mobile home air conditioning is an absolute necessity, inside temperatures can sometimes get high even with air conditioning. This puts a heavy load on cooling equipment and makes for big electric bills. In these climates you want maximum reflection on the roof, even more than you get with aluminum pigmentation. For this, there are available super-white roof coatings, one with fiber, one without. The non-fibrous is for roofs that have already been fiber coated, but where the owner later decides he wants more reflection. The fibrous white is for new homes with uncoated roofs, or for old previously coated ones that are ready for a re-coat job.

THE BEST WAY TO COAT A ROOF

I checked around my park for opinions on what was the best way to coat a roof. The consensus was that it's a stinking job and is best done sitting in the shade with a cold can of beer watching some kid do it for ten bucks. However, if you can't arrange this, the best way to do it depends on what you are coating the roof *with*.

With non-fibrated super-white, thickness of the coating is not important. All you want is a cover of white for reflection. A roller will give you fast and economical coverage. The commercial cost-cutting outfits use a roller on everything because they get twice the coverage out of a 5-gallon bucket. This is nice for *them*.

With the fibrous coatings, a roller lays it on too thin. It is better to lay it down heavy with a cheap throw-away brush (Fig. 6-8). These are inexpensive brushes you can buy in any paint store, including the removable handles. The purpose of a "fibrous" coating is not looks, but insulation and sound deadening. You just can't accomplish this by spreading it on thin "to save money." So lay it down, brushing mainly in one direction. Don't over-brush. This makes for a rough appearance.

The same throw-away brush can be used for blacktopping your driveway. You can also roll, but this will depend on what you use. Plain blacktop sealer is fairly thin, or can be further thinned so it will roll on. But sealer-filler is heavy and should *not* be thinned.

THE BEST WAY TO BLACKTOP A DRIVEWAY

Some paint store salesman will try to sell you a squeegee or a squeegee-brush combination. A squeegee on the roof is useless. There are too many dips and hollows. On your driveway, the

Fig. 6-8. An inexpensive brush, removable from the extension handle, can be purchased in any paint store and is thrown away when you finish. Handbrushing this job can lead to a painful backache. Don't try to improve on the above method—trial and error has proven it to be the cheapest, easiest, and best way.

squeegee could give you fits. This tool is not for amateurs because in trying to work it two directions, forwards and backwards, that squeegee blade will flip blacktop in all directions. Amateurs with a squeegee end up with blacktop specks on the home, the utility building, the skirting, the snow wall—even the dog and their kids. The blacktop specks dry almost instantly and then it takes days of tedious work with tar remover to clean up the mess. Warning: stay away from squeegees!

Blacktop sealer-filler, like fibrous roof coating, is best laid down easily with the same throw-away brush. This brush, once it is soaked, will not splatter. This is not true of a roller. If you work it too fast, it *will* splatter.

If you do make a mess, you want a blacktop material that is quickly and easily cleaned. Think about this when you buy. There are two basic types, the water base and the petroleum distillates base. That last is just a fancy term for turpentine. With the distillate base types, you thin and clean up with turpentine or paint thinner. This material has a high gloss to it, and looks the same dry as it does when you put it on. You never know when it's dry until you touch it. Sometimes it takes days to dry. This can be very important consideration if you have children or pets to worry about keeping off the driveway. This type you should roll on in a thin coat to speed drying. Otherwise you'll be parking your cars out on the street for weeks and getting nasty little notes from the park manager about Rule 24.

The water base blacktop material thins and cleans up with water. It dries fast in hot weather (July-August is the best time) and you actually *see* it drying as it gradually loses the wet glossy look and takes on a dull, flat sheen. Within an hour you can walk on it. While your wife is out shopping with the kids, you can have the driveway coated and dry when they get back but only to walk on. It takes about two days before you can drive over it. With a soft brush on the end of a long stick, you can't possibly foul up with the water base material, unless you step in the bucket.

If your driveway is getting a first coat, if it is gray looking and little stones are visible, you should use a filler-sealer because sealer alone will disappear into weathered asphalt like ink into a blotter. On future re-coats, sealer alone will be enough.

FIXING DAMAGED DRIVEWAYS

Filler is also called for if your driveway has cracks, holes or other small damaged areas. For major damage caused by frost and engine drippings, a bituminous mix must be used. This is basically the same stuff that state and county maintenance departments use to fill in potholes.

Do the repair work before you blacktop. Clean all loose dirt out of the hole. For better adhesion, paint a little sealer around in the hole before you fill it with the mix. You can tamp it down by foot, or even drive over it with a front wheel of your car, if you can find something smooth like a piece of plywood to protect it from tire grooves. When the patched areas cure in a few days, you can then coat the entire driveway, and the repaired areas will be barely noticeable, except to professional nit-pickers like retired building inspectors.

If you live in cold weather country, don't try to save for next year any left-over blacktop sealer, if it is of the water base type. It will freeze. Instead, use it up with a second coat. Put it on your neighbor's driveway. Or blacktop a space the size of your car directly in front of your home. This will utterly confound the park manager. He will suspect you plan to park your car on this space. He will drive past your home every night for a month checking up on you. Then he'll question the neighbors. He'll go crazy trying to figure out *why* you blacktopped that space in the street.

FIXING UTILITY BUILDING RUST AND LEAKS

Steel utility buildings, a fixture beside all mobile homes, are a plague invented by the Devil and a consortium of rolled steel fabricators to befoul the environment with rust and ugliness. The buildings look seductively beautiful in the Sears and Ward's catalogs, with beautiful models in hot pants posing on rider-mowers. But in less than one year of weathering beside your home, that building will be a hideous eyesore of rusty screwheads and panels, noisy roofs and sticking doors that either won't open, or break loose at the bottom and bang against the building.

On windy days, steel utility buildings frequently take off and look like some strange object from outer space. In fact, this could very likely be what many people see and report as another UFO. Last October, during a wind storm of up to 70-mile gusts, I saw a 10

Fig. 6-9. Kool Seal roof coating, in both fibrated and non-fibrated, is an excellent protective cover for steel utility buildings. With conventional paints, the rust soon bleeds through, but if you apply a thick dab of fibrated coating over the rusted screws and panel ends, the rust will stay covered.

× 10 building take off like a Boeing 727 to a height of about 200 feet, fly through the air about 500 yards, and crash land on top of a utility pole.

I have two of these buildings, but mine are completely protected from the weather by a 70-foot all enclosed carport. Even with this protection, some of the screwheads are rusting. If your building is exposed to the weather, as most are, and if it leaks badly, as most do, the "Miracle Seal" tape is perfect for the job. Utility building leaks are impossible to fix with conventional caulking methods and materials because most of the leaks are caused by windblown rain. Water hitting the sides of the building comes in over the top of panels to the inside wall, then runs down to the floor. The top endings of all panels should be covered with strips of the rolled tape.

Roof leaks are always through the rusted screwheads. These can be fixed in either of two ways: cover all the screwheads with 2½ inch squares of the rubber tape, then a thick coat of fibrated roof coating; or cover all the screws with a dab of fibrated roof coating, then coat the entire roof.

The super-white Kool Seal roof coating (Fig. 6-9) is also excellent for covering the entire building. With ordinary non-fibrated paint, rust will eventually bleed through, especially on the ends of panels. Steel utility buildings are unbearably hot in the summer. This is another good reason for using the super white reflective cover.

For further information on the products mentioned in this chapter, write to:

Miracle Seal

Revere Chemical Corporation
30875 Carter Street
Solon, Ohio 44139

Kool Seal (also makers of Quiet Roof)

The Electric Paint & Varnish Co.
8001 Franklin Blvd.,
Cleveland, Ohio 44102

Save With 7
Proper Setup and
Maintenance

One of the biggest myths of mobile home living is that it is "carefree." This is one of the industry's biggest selling points and hooks many buyers who have had it with the painting, the grass cutting, the leaf raking, the snow removal and the endless one-mil levies on real estate. "There's always something on a house that needs fixing," they wail.

So when these disgruntled property owners accept a firm offer on their homes, and while they're waiting for the closing, they immediately have a garage sale, and anything connected with work goes on the block. Who needs a power lawnmower? A hedge trimmer? A snow blower? An electric drill? Who *needs* twenty different screwdrivers? So everything is marked down to sell. And it does. And immediately, after moving into a mobile home, all those things that were sold have to be replaced.

Warning: don't sell *anything*!

NEW TOOLS YOU WILL NEED

Although I had been warned, and didn't make the mistake of selling all my tools, I still had to buy new ones that I had never even needed before. For example, who needs a screwjack? Who needs masonry drill bits in all sizes? Who needs a line level, or a clutch screwdriver? I didn't even know what the last two things *were*. They had to be explained to me. I still don't understand a clutch screw.

Drills

Although I already owned two electric drills in ¼ and ½ inch sizes, I still had to buy two new ones, the variable-speed reversible full-torque drills for driving and removing screws. Incidently, when you buy such a drill (and you *will*) be sure it's full torque. This is very important. "Full torque" means full power at *all* speeds. With most variable speed drills, when you reduce speed to drive a Phillips head screw, you also reduce power. As a result, there is not enough power left to drive the screw. But when you step up the power to drive the screw, the Phillips bit jumps out of the screwhead and chews it up so bad you have to back it out with pliers. When you're putting up a utility building or carport, driving thousands of screws, this can be very aggravating and could cause you to use profane words in the presence of your children. Don't *ever* buy such a drill unless it has full torque. Variable speed is a meaningless thing if you can't use it. You absolutely *must* have a power tool that will drive and remove screws. Mobile homes are put together with billions of sheetmetal screws. If you try to remove them manually, your arm will fall off.

Clutch Screws and Screwdrivers

A tool that you will need almost the moment you walk in the front door of your new home is a clutch screwdriver. This is a specialty item peculiar to the mobile home industry. It is almost impossible to describe a clutchhead screw, so I won't try. Just look at the picture (Fig. 7-1). Until I bought a mobile home, I had never seen such a screw, and didn't even know what to ask for at a small country store. I tried to describe it and everybody stared at me like I had one eye in the middle of my forehead. I got mad and walked out.

You absolutely *must* have this screwdriver, as you will quickly learn after moving into your new home and noticing that everything in the place is fastened down with crazy looking screws. This is a fastener that was designed for high speed production and power tools. Chief source of supply for the mobile home industry is the United Screw & Bolt Corporation, 3590 West 58th Street, Cleveland, Ohio 44102. This company also makes power bits in all types and sizes for this fastener.

Before learning about this company, I made my own bits by buying four extra screwdrivers in various sizes, hacksawing off the ends, flattening the shafts on a grindstone, then using them as bits in my electric drills. But you will still need at least three hand

Fig. 7-1. You will see this peculiar screwhead all through the inside and outside of your mobile home. On quick glance, the clutch fastening looks like an Allen screw, which it is not. It is designed to be power-driven in high-speed production work.

screwdrivers for those little odd jobs around the house that require the removal of only one or two clutch screws.

If you live in or near a large city, check the Yellow Pages under mobile homes. Specialty firms that service the mobile home trade will definitely have clutch screwdrivers. Next, look under tools, but call first. Last, try the big hardware stores.

Warning: take a sample screw with you. Pull out a few drawers. Look under the kitchen sink, way back in the dark corners You will find sawdust, pieces of lumber, linoleum, an empty Alka Selzer bottle, candy wrappers, a wad of chewing tobacco. You will also sweep up a big handful of sheetmetal screws and skinny finishing nails. Why so many? Why are they there? Why chewing tobacco?

In factory production lines, high-paid workers are forbidden to pick up anything they drop. Once anything hits the floor, it's garbage. To mobile home manufacturers, it is more economical to let dropped items lie then have assembly line production slowed while a worker stops to pick up a fastener or something else he drops. And in highspeed production, screws and nails are constantly being dropped.

Mobile homes are held together by sheetmetal screws, skinny finishing nails, multi-pronged staples and spit. That's right, spit! In some places, workers in the mobile home factories chew tobacco. When putting up plywood wall panels, they sometimes spit on the studs before zapping the panel with an air gun that drives colored finishing nails. I could get no explanation for this. Perhaps the tobacco spit holds the thin panel in place until it is zapped.

Buying a Clutch Screwdriver

Take a sample clutch screw with you to the hardware store and lots of luck. The eager young lady who rushed up to wait on me must have just started her day clerking in a hardware store. I handed her the sample screw. "I want a clutch screwdriver to fit that."

She walked away, stopped, studied a moment, and came back. "You want a *what* for this?"

I told her again and she walked away mumbling to herself. She came back five minutes later with an older man who looked like movie actor Percy Kilbride of those Ma and Pa Kettle pictures. He even talked like him.

He said, "You the man who lives in a trailer?"

Should something similar happen to you, don't say anything sarcastic and further tarnish the image we mobile homers inherited from those ugly trailer parks with the oil drums on 2 × 4 stands. People still tend to look down their noses at us. This is where you can help upgrade that image, like I did when I said pleasantly, "I do not live in a trailer, sir."

"Doesn't this screw come from . . . "

"A trailer, sir, is something you hook up to the back of car and then pull up to Devil's Lake for a weekend of fishing. I live in a manufactured home."

He looked confused. "What kind of a home did you say?"

"Manufactured. They used to be called mobile homes."

"Oh, them."

I didn't like the way he said that. "Sir, did you know that the government is projecting figures of some 50 million Americans living in manufactured homes by 1980? That adds up to millions of clutch screwdrivers."

He thought about this a moment. "I better order some."

You will hear something like that many times before you finally locate a store that stocks clutch screwdrivers and then only in one size. You should have at least three sizes—6, 8, and 10— because each tool fits *only* one size screw. All the covers on your electric wall outlets have brown clutch screws with No. 6 heads.

All door hinges are held on with No. 8, and all your exterior siding screws are No. 10.

REPLACING RUSTED SIDING SCREWS

My neighbor, with nothing better to do one day, estimated there were nine million clutch screws on the outside of my home, and half of them were rusty. He only said that because he knew it would upset me and because I told him the moles in my lawn were moving over to his lawn.

A week later, I received a little note with my rent bill reminding me of Park Rule 19, which proclaims that mobile homes must be washed down regularly and kept clean of rust streaks. So each day now I remove a few dozen rusted screws, and replace them with stainless steel. Wanda used my little calculator to figure out how long it would take me to replace all the screws. She said at 3 dozen a day, and assuming there really were nine million in our home, it would take me about 675 years to replace all of them.

Some manufacturers (very few) eliminate this problem by using only stainless steel siding screws. The custom builders use them, but only if the buyer requests stainless steel. If you have this option, insist on it no matter how much it costs extra. If you don't, you will only have to replace them all yourself as they rust and ruin the appearance of your home—and at great expense because stainless steel is very expensive.

The clutch head is not available in stainless steel. So I am replacing mine with slot heads. I don't like Phillips screws because I built a boat once with them and almost went out of my mind chewing up the soft brass heads with a power screwdriver.

It was because of the siding screws that I bought two variable-speed reversing full-torque drills. I use one for clutch screws coming out, the other for stainless steel going in. With only one drill, I would be constantly changing bits back and forth.

Of all the power tools made, the electric drill is the most useful to a homeowner. And the most useful of all drills is the cordless type. I bought one of the first new Black & Decker cordless drills over 10 years ago and have virtually worn it out with constant use. It has been recharged a thousand times and still has the original batteries. You will find hundreds of uses for a cordless drill, especially when you're working under your home, up on the roof, or on a ladder when a long wire is not only a nuisance but a safety hazard.

If you live in a small town and can find no source of supply for stainless steel sheetmetal screws, here are four companies who manufacture them:

ITT Harper, Inc,
8200 Lehigh Avenue
Morton Grove, Illinois
Rockford Products Corp.
Rockford, Illinois 61101

Metal Products Company, Inc.
Castleton-On-Hudson, New York
Russell, Burdsall & Ward
R.B.W. Bolt & Nut Company
Mentor, Ohio

ANCHORAGE OF MOBILE HOMES

Many states (21) have some sort of code requiring the anchorage of mobile homes, or are making studies and introducing new legislation. It is only a matter of time until it will be mandatory in all 50 states and insurance companies will refuse to honor damage claims where the home was not properly secured. It's the same way with seat belts. Police filling out accident forms in Ohio today ask: "Were you wearing your seat belt?" If you answer no, many insurance companies operating in this state will not fully honor injury claims. You'll get the same run-around with mobile home claims. There will be a question on every damage report: "Was home anchored in accordance with state codes?" If you answer no, you will be living in a motel room for a long time waiting for a settlement, finally getting only a fraction of what you are entitled to. As some Chinese philosopher once said, "Is not necessary to ride in elevator to get shaft." Just give an insurance company a loophole.

One manufacturer of anchoring systems uses this scare copy in his advertising: "A leading university study has revealed that 60 mph wind gusts can topple a mobile home, destroying it and most of the possessions, and possibly inflicting severe injury to the occupants. U.S. Weather Bureau statistics reveal that all areas of the country have at one time or another been subjected to at least 60 mph winds. In one year alone, over 5,000 mobile homes were toppled by winds in America, not including the hurricane zone."

The advertisement does not give the name of the "leading university" that made the study, but the facts and statistics are true. I personally have seen a mobile home that was toppled off its blocks by 45 mph winds. Yet, I have seen others that were hit by 80 mph gusts and didn't move an inch, including my own.

Insurance companies and local building authorities are behind most of the codes and regulations requiring the anchorage of mobile homes. As one salesman told me, "If the insurance companies won't insure, the banks won't lend money for mortgages, and

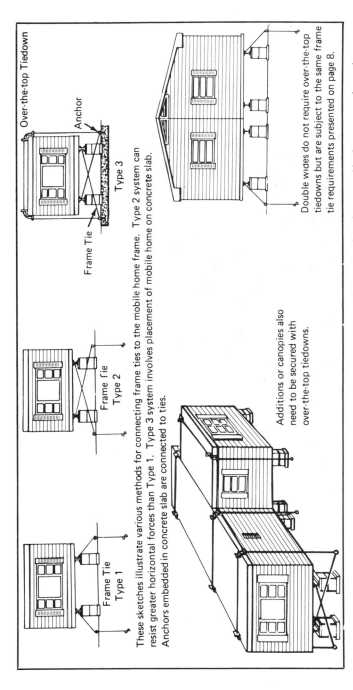

Over-the-top Tiedown

Frame Tie

Type 3

Anchor

Frame Tie
Type 2

Frame Tie
Type 1

These sketches illustrate various methods for connecting frame ties to the mobile home frame. Type 2 system can resist greater horizontal forces than Type 1. Type 3 system involves placement of mobile home on concrete slab. Anchors embedded in concrete slab are connected to ties.

Additions or canopies also need to be secured with over-the-top tiedowns.

Double wides do not require over-the-top tiedowns but are subject to the same frame tie requirements presented on page 8.

Fig. 7-2. Various methods to tie down your mobile home. If you screw your anchor augers into the ground in the manner shown here, you will have problems with straps or chains running through your skirting. It's more work to screw the augers down under the home, but it will look better.

145

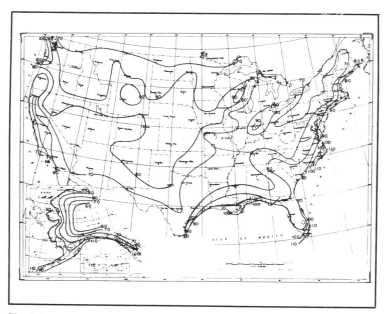

Fig. 7-3. National wind map, showing the maximum gust velocities that you can expect in your area. When tying down, you should plan for the worst gusts, of course, and not just the regular winds.

suddenly people in Indiana, Alabama, and California are applying for unemployment checks.

Manufacturers, sellers and parks are getting the message and today all mobile homes are coming from the factory with steel straps hanging down their sides, which puzzled me the first time I saw them.

"They're for anchoring," I was told by a set-up foreman.

The great majority of mobile homes in this country are *not* anchored, especially in those parks which do not provide a concrete pad or ribbons. New parks today provide four steel loops set in the concrete for anchoring, which simplify the job. Without these loops there is considerably more work and expense involved. If you are in one of those homes not yet anchored, you can do the job yourself.

Where to Buy Anchoring Accessories

One good source of approved anchoring equipment is *Minute Man Anchors*, 305 West Walker Street, East Flat Rock, North Carolina 28726. The Sears Roebuck Mobile Home Accessories Catalog also lists this equipment, with two different systems for homes sitting on a concrete base, and two for homes sitting directly on the ground.

Types of Tiedowns

In Fig. 7-2 you will see the various types of tiedowns. Fig. 7-3 is a national wind map. In Fig. 7-4 you determine from the chart what your tiedown requirements will be. In Fig. 7-5 you have the option of using cable or strap, and in some cases chain under the home. You tighten the cable with turnbuckles. The steel strap you tighten with a wrench on those special tension head bolts.

On Concrete

On a concrete tiedown, holes must be drilled for setting the appropriate slab anchors, either with an eye head for a turnbuckle, or a tension head for strap.

On the Ground

If your home sits directly on the ground, you will use earth anchors (Fig. 7-6) which come with three different heads. If you plan on using over-the-top tiedowns, you will set the auger-anchors just beyond the edge of your home as in Fig. 7-2. This is awkward with skirting. If you don't plan on using over-the-top tiedowns, you can set your earth anchors under your home and not mess up your

Wind velocity m.p.h.	10- and 12- ft.- wide mobile homes				12- and 14-ft.-wide mobile homes	
	30 to 50 ft. long		50 to 60 ft. long		60 to 70 ft. long	
	No. of ** frame ties	No. of over-the-top ties	No. of ** frame ties	No. of over-the-top ties	No. of ** frame ties	No. of over-the-top ties
70	3	2	4	2	4	2
80	4	3	5	3	5	3
90	5	4	6	4	7	4
100	6	5	7	5	8	6
110	7	6	9	6	10	7

*Tiedown components used must be able to withstand at least 4,750 lb. without failure. Anchors capable of withstanding 5,700 lb. without failure also are required. The molding power of ground anchors can be determined by conducting pullout tests or by consulting with your anchor dealer. He should be able to provide you with data on anchor holding power for various kinds of solids.

**The number of frame ties shown is based on using the Type 2 frame the system (p. 7) which can resist a greater horizontal force than Type 1. If Type 1 frame ties are used, the quantity shown in the table should be increased by one additional tie.

Fig. 7-4. Table of tiedown anchorage requirements.

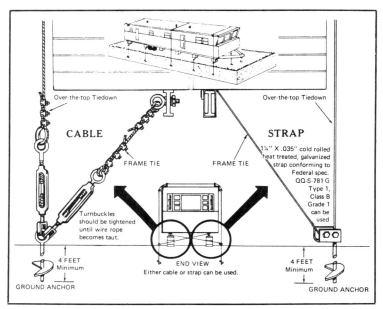

Fig. 7-5. Although not shown in this drawing, chain can be used, but only under the home. The over-the-roof tiedown is rarely seen except on small homes in hurricane country because it is so unsightly.

skirting. However, this will make it a little more difficult getting the anchor into the ground because they are about 50 inches long and you haven't got that much headroom. You have to hand-dig a starting hole at least two feet deep, work the auger into the hole, then screw it down the rest of the way. Then you fill in the hole with dirt and tamp it down hard with a short length of 2 × 4 and a hammer. Secure the anchor to the I-beam with whatever you have decided on, strap, cable or chain.

These earth anchors are actually far better than some of the tiedowns provided in many parks where they use tension straps secured to U-rods set in concrete ribbons. These ribbons are nothing more than 20-inch strips of concrete the thickness of a 2 × 4 lying on top of the ground. In the Xenia, Ohio tornado disaster, mobile homes were lifted up off the ground along with their ribbons. Mobile homes secured to earth anchors were still there, even though minus a carport and awnings.

ANCHORING AWNINGS

Awnings are especially vulnerable to wind, and not necessarily strong winds. In my park, when awnings are blown away I always investigate to find out why. In every case it is due to improper installation. Putting it bluntly, if an awning is properly installed, it will not blow off, except in winds of hurricane force.

In less than three months after a porch canopy was installed over my side emergency exit door, it blew off in only 35 mph winds and crashed into another home 200 yards away. When I investigated, I found that the two support columns had not been secured to the cement steps on which they rested. The columns took off with the awning which, at the sides, were fastened to the home with 1-inch sheetmetal screws going into thin aluminum siding and fiberglass insulation. There was no wood behind that siding for the screws to go into. You could have pulled those screws out of that thin aluminum with your teeth.

When I showed this to the owner of the company that manufactured and installed the awning, he just laughed and repeated an old cliche: "You just can't get good help these days."

I laughed too, but I didn't think it was so funny when he billed me for repairing the awning. He became annoyed when I refused to permit his workmen to re-install the awning canopy. I did it myself and I did it *right*. It has since been subjected to 70 mph wind gusts, and it is still there.

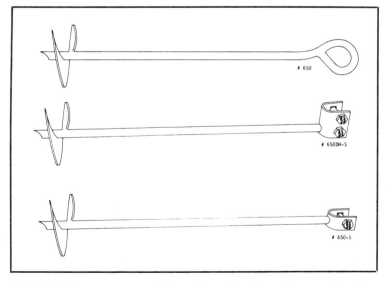

Fig. 7-6. Anchor augers come in three types. Top: Auger for use with chain or cable. Middle: Auger for steel straps running both over the top and under the home. Bottom: Auger for single strap frame tiedown.

The company that installed my canopy is considered the best. It has the highest reputation, and the highest prices. I don't like to think what the other companies are doing. Yet I hear about it every time we have a wind storm, such as the one last fall when a widow lost her entire home in one short second.

Patios Improperly Anchored

A large patio cover was the cause of this total disaster. Six aluminum support columns, holding up the 20 × 16 foot roof, pulled up out of the concrete pad, and the whole mess took off. The home and patio area faced west, with nothing to break the wind for a distance of about 200 feet. On the day of disaster, the winds were WSW and gusting at 60 mph.

With the passing of sailing vessels, only us weekend sailors understand and appreciate the dynamic forces generated by wind, once the only source of power for ships that moved the commerce of the world. The large surface area of a carport or patio roof becomes like a sail in high winds from certain angles. A gust of wind hit that mobile home at precisely the right angle, creating tremendous upward pressures which pulled the patio support posts right out of the concrete foundation. The roof swung up, the 16-foot panels exerting powerful leverage at the point where they were fastened to the home.

Archimedes once said, "Give me a lever long enough and a place to stand and I can move the earth."

What a Patio Roof Can Do

The leverage force, as the patio panels swung up and over, was strong enough to rip out the wood to which it and all the roof trusses of the home were fastened. As the panels blew over the home, they peeled off the steel roof like the skin on a banana, taking all the roof trusses with it. The whole mess landed with a tremendous crash on the ground between two other homes. And the widow, home alone, looked up and saw stars in the sky. It was all over in a second.

There was much publicity in the area newspapers, and much local comment on how easily a mobile home could be completely demolished. "Mobile homes are nothing but crackerboxes!" one said bitterly.

I heard the same comment last summer when a young couple, with three pre-school children, lost their mobile home to fire. One woman said, "Mobile homes are firetraps."

I personally investigated both of the above tragedies because I, too, am deeply involved in the mobile home way of life. When something like this happens, I want to know *why*. The fire was caused by the three little children who had been home alone and had been playing in a dark clothes closet with matches. It is unfair to call mobile homes "fire traps" because matches in the hands of children can start a fire anywhere. Mrs. O'Leary's cow kicked over a lantern and burned down Chicago.

WHY DISASTERS HAPPEN

The cause of the roof disaster I found in the patio concrete pad—12 little screw holes out on the edge where the patio aluminum support posts had been fastened down. I was stunned when I saw those 12 tiny holes, about 3/16 inch, two for each post. I have never seen a masonry drill or lead anchors in such a small size. The holes were drilled apparently with an ordinary steel bit.

When I checked the aluminum posts in the wreckage, one of them still had a screw stuck in the bracket at the base. It was a 1-inch No. 12 sheetmetal screw. That was all! No lead anchor, just that small screw driven directly into concrete.

When I questioned one of the neighbors, he said, "Two kids came out one morning in a van and worked all day putting up the patio cover."

He remembered so well because they had a radio in the van playing at peak volume and it woke him up. He works nights and normally sleeps until noon, and he was annoyed. Watching them work, he had gotten the impression they didn't really know what they were doing because they had so much trouble interlocking the roof panels together and sliding them up to the side of the home. They would stick half way up, and the kids would hammer on the ends with a piece of wood and damage the panels. Then they would laugh as they worked to straighten them with pliers.

The above is not an isolated case, but typical of what to expect from many companies who work in, or rather who exploit the mobile home field.

THE EXPLOITERS

Usually there will be just two firms in any specific classification, from TV repair to pizza deliveries, who have exclusive rights to work (exploit) a park. You are a captive customer and have no choice but to do business with them. If you don't like it, you do the work yourself. If you have already done business with them, you better start checking on those awnings, carports, patio covers, and porch enclosures. You might wake up some night looking at stars in the sky.

What to Look For

The top of your awning, where it is fastened over the window to a hinge-like strip of aluminum, is rarely a problem, except for leaking dirty water down over the windows. It is where the sides are fastened to the siding that trouble occurs (Fig. 7-7). If you specifically ordered an awning wider than the window itself, which many do, the sides will be beyond the window or door frame, as you can see in the picture. This means there is no stud, no wood to which the sides can be secured.

When this happens, the boys in the vans just drill a screw hole through the siding *between* the studs and secure the awning sides to nothing but flimsy aluminum. In every incident I investigated where an awning blew off, this was the reason.

So what do you do if you find that your awnings have been installed in this shoddy manner? Do you assume the attitude that this is for the insurance companies to worry about? Like one man said, "I signed a contract with Northwest Awning. I paid them by check. It's *their* problem. Let the things blow off. That's why I got insurance."

There is just one thing wrong with the above. Sometimes when awnings go sailing through the air, they damage more then just aluminum. Sometimes they damage people. That's what happened in a Florida park when an awning crashed through a window and injured a sleeping baby in a crib. How does the insurance pay *that* off?

The Price of Security

So what do you do if you find awnings, patios, and carports held down with screws that you can pull out with your fingers? You can be a man of principle, or you can fix them yourself. Your biggest investment will be time and labor. The cost for materials—bolts, lag screws, lead anchors, aluminum tubing—will be a small price to pay for security and peace of mind.

If your patio, or carport supports, rest directly on a concrete foundation, they should be held down either with ½ inch lag screws into ⅝ lead anchors or ¼ inch bolts set in anchoring cement as in Fig. 7-8 and Fig. 7-9. If your patio foundation is at least 10 × 15 in size, it will hold down that roof.

Fig. 7-7. The sides of this awning extend beyond the door framing where there is no stud. It is fastened to nothing but aluminum siding, a common reason that so many awnings blow away. Note that this owner is holding his awning down with aluminum tubing screwed to the door frame.

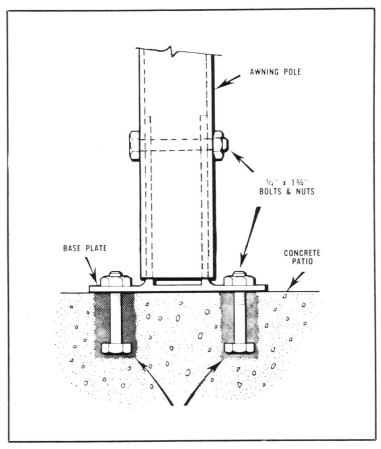

AWNING POLE

¼" x 1¾"
BOLTS & NUTS

BASE PLATE

CONCRETE PATIO

Fig. 7-8. Here is where disaster begins—the base plate on every patio or carport roof. If the base plate is not properly anchored, in high winds a light aluminum roof, like a ship's sail, can exert enough power to take off.

ANCHORING CARPORTS

Carport columns are rarely set on a cement driveway because most mobile home driveways are either asphalt or crushed stone. If the driveway extends beyond where the columns will sit, square hole are usually cut through the asphalt and down at least 24 inches, depending on the frost line for your section of the country.

Some installers will come to your home a few days in advance to dig these holes, fill them with concrete and imbed bolts. Others will just put the columns down into the holes and pour concrete right over them.

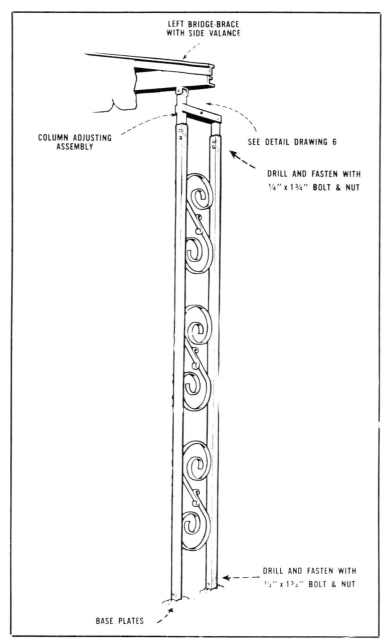

LEFT BRIDGE-BRACE
WITH SIDE VALANCE

COLUMN ADJUSTING
ASSEMBLY

SEE DETAIL DRAWING 6

DRILL AND FASTEN WITH
¼″ x 1¾″ BOLT & NUT

DRILL AND FASTEN WITH
¼″ x 1¾″ BOLT & NUT

BASE PLATES

Fig. 7-9. Carport or patio support.

Allow for Tearing Down

I prefer the first method because if and when you move someday, you will be tearing down the carport, taking it with you. The aluminum columns installed by the first method will be easy to remove by just digging down a few inches to reach the imbedded bolts. In the second method you must dig up that heavy mass of concrete stuck to the base of the column.

Remember this if you decide to put up your own carport. Both of the above methods are good, but you must allow for the possibility you may move some day, to another park, another town, another state. It happens every day. That is why there are so many transport companies in 50 states who do nothing else but move mobile homes.

Never Leave a Carport

Perhaps the thought crosses your mind that it might be simpler to just leave the carport behind for the next tenant. Perhaps you would like to have bills follow you to your next address. The park will only tear down your carport and bill you for the labor. If you ignore them, the bill will be turned over to a national collection agency who is affiliated with a local agency who has an employee who lives in your new park. This is no joke. You find these people everywhere. There are two men and a woman living in my park who work for collection agencies—another one of the many hats worn by "private detectives," "investigators," and "research consultants."

The Price of Carports

As to just walking away from a carport, have you priced one recently? A typical 40 foot carport with 16 foot projection and 5 foot privacy or snow wall will cost around $3,500 installed. My 70 foot all enclosed carport would cost over $7,000 to replace at today's aluminum prices. You just don't walk away from that kind of money, and then pay somebody else to tear down and resell.

Why Carport Roofs Blow Away

The first year after my park opened, six carport roofs blew away—but only the roofs. The aluminum columns remained. What happened?

The weak link in carport installations is at the top of the columns where they support the roof (Fig. 7-10). Note that the fastening here is a bolt and nut; that is, it is *supposed* to be a nut and

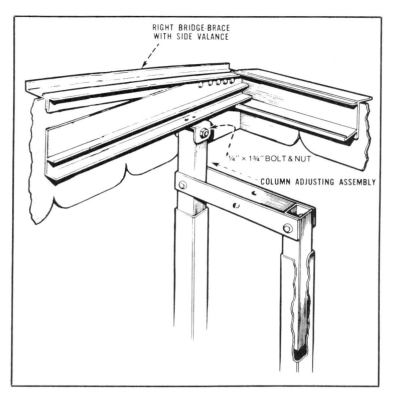

RIGHT BRIDGE-BRACE
WITH SIDE VALANCE

¼" × 1¾" BOLT & NUT

COLUMN ADJUSTING ASSEMBLY

Fig. 7-10. This is another point where disasters begin. Commercial awning and carport installers frequently substitute a cheap sheetmetal screw for the ¼-inch bolt which holds the roof to the support column.

bolt with lock washer. Many installers substitute lag screws in this critical area, and that is why those six roofs blew away.

Why Screws Fall Out

In any point of contact between two pieces of metal which is exposed to wind and weather, there is constant movement. You can't see this movement, but it's going on all the time when the wind blows—a wiggling, shifting motion which gradually enlarges holes in metal. As the holes get larger, the screws slowly work out. This is what happened to me when I put up additional braces on my awning. I used sheetmetal screws and in less then two weeks they all fell out. I replaced them all with bronze bolts and lock washers. Since bronze lock washers are hard to find in a non-seaport community, you can instead use two brass nuts, and tighten them

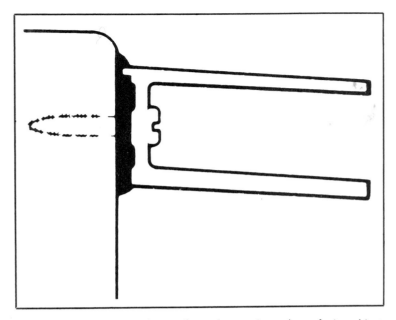

Fig. 7-11. This is how awning, patio, and carport panels are fastened to a home—the wrong way. The panels just fit into that groove and are screwed down on the bottom side. If a patio or carport with this type bracket rips off, it can take the home roof right along with it.

against each other. This is how boat propellors are locked on their shafts.

In the six carport roofs that blew away, ¼ × 2 inch sheetmetal screws had been used instead of that bolt and nut. These screws slowly backed out of the enlarged holes and there was nothing holding those roofs down but the law of gravity.

How Carports are Fastened to a Home

Now, when those six carport roofs blew away, why didn't they peel off the roof of the mobile home, as happened with the widow? Look closely at Fig. 7-11 and Fig. 7-12. You see here the two different ways patios, awnings, carports are attached to a home. Fig. 7-12 is a hinged coupling. Fig. 7-11 is a fixed hook-up. The roof panels slide into that U-channel and are held with screws on the bottom. On the hinged coupling in Fig. 7-12, the carport roof can easily swing up and pull right out of that round channel attached to the house with no damage. But in the fixed hook-up Fig. 7-11, when the carport roof swings up, it rips off the edge of the home and takes everything with it. This is what happened to the widow's home. Yet even after all these casualties and insurance claims, carport, patios, and awnings are still being installed in the same way.

Most of the people in the aluminum awning business work in a manner that suits their convenience and work schedules. Anything that slows them up they discard. They all use hex-head fastenings because they can be driven with power tools. Bolts and nuts cannot be power driven. It is a slow manual job with a wrench and a screwdriver, so they substitute a big screw for the bolt. Of course, as long as the insurance company pays the casualty claim, you can just leave it that way. But think again about that baby in the crib and that big carport roof flying around in a crowded community. Replacing those 2 × 2 inch screws with bolts, nuts and lock washers is so easy and inexpensive.

HOW TO SECURE AWNINGS

Your awnings, to be made wind-proof, will require additional bracing supports as in Fig. 7-7. You make these supports out of

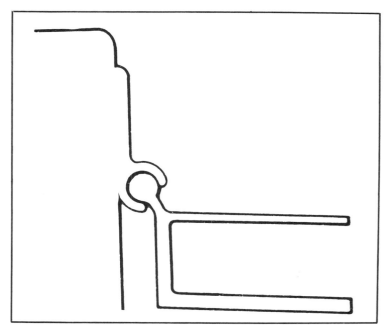

Fig. 7-12. A much superior and commonly used method of attaching carport and patio panels to homes. The roof can pull out of this hinge easily without destroying your home.

Fig. 7-13. This is Sears Roebuck's hurricane awning. The L-shaped rod in the bracket pulls out and the awning swings down to cover the window, protecting it from flying debris and making the awning less vulnerable.

aluminum tubing, which you can buy in most any hardware store that sells aluminum for do-it-yourself projects. Both ends of the tubing are squeezed flat in a vice, then bent to whatever angle is required. Then you drill ¼ holes through the flat ends for your fastenings. Where the tubing attaches to the awning, use only a brass bolt and two nuts. On the house side, where you are going directly into wood, you can use a 1-½ inch No. 10 sheetmetal screw. Don't worry, it is only in metal-to-metal where screws work loose and fall out.

HURRICANE AWNINGS

If you live in hurricane sections of the country, Sears Roebuck sells a very fine awning which not only looks good and is easy to install, but has a novel extra feature. With hurricane warnings up, this awning can be quickly detached at the support post, (Fig. 7-13) and dropped down to cover the window. In this position it is not only less vulnerable to wind, but also protects the window from flying debris.

Even in non-hurricane country, it is still a very fine awning and can be adjusted to three different heights, another extra feature. There is just one bracket (Fig. 7-12) to screw down across the top of your window. With your wife holding one end, you guide the other end into that round track on the bracket. Small post brackets (Fig. 7-13) are secured to the side window framing, where you are certain to hit solid wood. The awning is raised and the aluminum posts are locked into that bracket with those L-shaped rods at whatever height you choose. Note the brass bolt in the center of that rod with two locking nuts.

DO-IT-YOURSELF CARPORT

If you decide on a do-it-yourself carport or patio, write to the *Silvertop Manufacturing Company, Inc.*, of White Marsh, Maryland 21161. They have put together the most thorough and easy-to-understand instructions for a do-it-yourselfer that I have ever seen. You just can't go wrong with those huge step-by-step drawings. Also, their patio/carport roofs are the strongest I have ever seen (Fig. 7-14), which is extremely important if you live in big snow country.

THE IMPORTANCE OF A STRONG ROOF

Ohio is not normally big snow country. But last winter we had a freak 14-incher and in my park alone 23 carports collapsed down on top of cars, and countless awnings and patio roofs were dam-

Fig. 7-14. If you live in the north, you'll never have to worry about snow with this patio or carport roof. In the 1975 heavy snows, so many awnings, patios, and carports were damaged by snow that many insurance companies increased their rates with roofs that did not meet certain load specifications.

aged. In Buffalo, during that same snow storm, they had 30 inches of snow come in off the lake and nobody missed work and all the kids went to school, and not one single carport roof in a mobile home park was damaged. Why? Why did 14 inches of snow paralyze northwestern Ohio and cause millions in property damage, while Buffalo didn't even blink with 30 inches of snow?

The answer is that Buffalo is conditioned to *expect* 30 inches of snow, so they are prepared for it. Nobody would even think of buying a carport with roof panels that would buckle under the weight of a midget. In Buffalo they buy roofs like the one in Fig. 7-14. In Buffalo, the city uses the biggest and the best snow removal equipment.

In July when you are talking to a salesman about a carport, or materials for a do-it-yourself job, you don't think about snow. You just groan when you hear the quoted prices for 20 lb., 40 lb., and 60 lb. per square foot roof panels. This is the reason why so many mobile homers, trying to keep costs down, will settle for the 20 lb. panels. Always they regret later when they learn how fragile the 20 lb. panels really are. If you want to save on a carport, buy the best and put it up yourself.

In manual training, I was the dumbest kid in class. "How could you fail on book ends?" my mother asked.

If I can put up a carport, with just a wife's help, *anybody* can do it. If your wife is reading this book to you because you flunked out of third grade, don't let it bother you. You don't *have* to read. Just follow the step-by-step pictures in the huge drawings the Silvertop Company will send you. That's what I did.

Save With 8
the Right Lawn
and Landscaping

People are always asking me why I bought a mobile home. I tell them to get away from grass cutting. This utterly confuses them because usually when I am asked that dumb question, I am cutting the grass. In fact, I am always cutting the grass, or doing *something* to it. I work harder today on rented grass then I did when I owned grass. I still don't know exactly what happened. I only know that if you fertilize, you cut a lot of grass.

I never spent a dime on fertilizer in all my life until I bought a mobile home. I never used a grass catcher, just let the clippings lie. All trees looked alike to me. The same with weeds. I didn't even know what crabgrass was, even though everybody was talking about it all the time. Yet, in spite of this neglect and lack of interest on my part, I had one of the nicest lawns in the neighborhood. Which is why everybody hated me. They worked like dogs on their lawns, and I did absolutely nothing to mine but cut it. They all thought I had a secret. I did. I just didn't *care*. The minute you start to care about a lawn, you become a slave to it.

That is what has happened to me. The reason I care is because my neighbor has this fantastic lawn. Nobody knows how he does it.

There are about 1500 different kinds of grass in the United States. This is the first thing I learned when I began my research work on grass, and I think this figure should be corrected to 1501 because my neighbor has some rare hybrid. His grass seems to be a cross blend between Astro Turf and a fine fescues. He cuts it very short, about ½ inch, which in itself is remarkable because cool season grasses of the north just can't be cut that short in July and August. Yet, his grass never varies in appearance, always a deep, lush blue-green no matter how hot or dry the weather.

There is no fence between me and my grass freak neighbor and where our two lawns meet, the contrast is so striking that people will stop with squealing brakes to stare. By normal standards, I have what would be considered a fine lawn in my average neighborhood. But right next door to *his*, my lawn looks absolutely horrible. And people will drive away shaking their heads, feeling sorry for him because he lives next door to me.

This has had a traumatic emotional effect on me. I realized I had to shape up or move my home elsewhere. Remember this when you go lot hunting in mobile home parks. If you see a fantastic lawn, and an empty lot next to it, don't delude yourself into thinking that this would be a nice neighbor to have. That neighbor will become your mortal enemy in grass war. That is inevitably what happens and what happened to me. I have become a grass expert, an authority, a lawn freak. I was so much happier when I had that nice lawn on my own property and all the neighbors hated me.

THE START OF YOUR OWN LAWN

Having a nice lawn and well landscaped lot is easy, if you don't get involved in a grass war. If you buy a home in a quality park, a sodded lawn is usually part of a package deal which will include one or two trees, three evergreens and three shrubs. But most often you will put in your own lawn.

THE TWO MAJOR GRASS GROUPS

I mentioned 1500 types of grass, but actually only 40 of these are suitable for lawn cover. Even these are divided into a cool season group and a subtropical group. If you look at Fig. 8-1 you will see that the United States is divided into what is generally referred to as Kentucky Bluegrass country and Bermuda Grass country.

If you live along that dividing line, you will probably have a combination of both. Bermuda grass in Los Angeles looks like straw from December through March. So, in that dividing line from Santa Barbara, California across the country to Richmond, Virginia, mobile homeowners usually start to plant "winter grass" in their Bermuda lawns along about September through October. The purpose of this is to let the Perennial Rye(called "winter grass" in the south) take over during the Bermuda dormant season, hiding

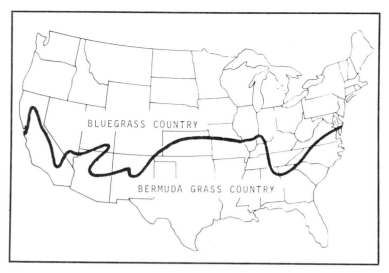

Fig. 8-1. Kentucky Bluegrass is the most popular of all lawn covers. Bermuda grass is second. Both Blue and Bermuda grasses are dormant during winter, but in the South, Bermuda's brown thatch is concealed by Perennial Rye, which is called "winter grass."

that ugly straw. In the spring, the situation is reversed as the Perennial Rye weakens and the Bermuda takes charge and makes a comeback. This keeps the lawn permanently green.

HOW TO PLANT "WINTER GRASS"

If you live in that subtropical Bermuda belt, there are many ways of doing this, and if gardening is your interest, you can make a career of doing nothing else. I will describe only the easy ways because lawn freaks already know all the hard ways.

You cut your Bermuda lawn short, usually about ¾ inch. This is not easy to do with power mowing, so professionals revert to the old reliable hand-powered reel mower, which will get you down close without scalping. Then you rake up all the dead grass and sow the rye seed.

The easy way to sow the seed is with a fertilizer spreader, preferably the cyclone type which will spin the seed out over a wider area than hopper type spreaders, and there is less chance of having those strips that you always miss no matter how careful you are. With the seed sown, you go back with the hand-powered reel mower and cut the grass again, but this time down to ½ inch, even closer if the mower can be set lower.

You leave these grass cuttings on the lawn this time as mulch and protective cover for the new seed. Then you water regularly, just as you would for a new lawn. When the rye starts to come up, you spread on a high nitrogen fertilizer, and your lawn will be green again until March, when Bermuda takes over.

COOL SEASON GRASSES

In that northern belt on the map, you have just the cool season grasses to contend with. Of this there are seven varieties in bluegrass, six in bent grass, four in fine fescues, two in rye, one in redtop, three in course fescues and one in clover.

The Coarse Fescues

All of the above grasses have their good points and bad ones. For example, the three coarse fescues are used mainly on football fields because they are wear resistant and bear up well under rough treatment. *Alta* and *Goars* are the two toughest in this group. *Meadow* is a medium coarse and not quite as wear resistant as the first two, but it has the highest survival rate as a "city" grass along sidewalks, in parks, and in areas of air pollution, smog, and dirt.

The Fine Fescues

These four grasses are not supposed to be used alone. They comprise a major portion of all blend mixtures. *Rainier* and *Chewings* are the two most commonly used because they are more tolerant of disease than *Illahee* and *Creeping Red*. Rainier is a dainty looking grass, soft deep green in appearance, which accounts for its popularity in all blends.

The Bent Grasses

All bents are high maintenance grasses and require constant attention, mowing, fertilizing, watering and disease control. It's like having another baby in the house. Three bents, *Penncross, Seaside* and *Congressional* must be kept mowed at ½ inch height which is almost impossible to do with a power mower unless you have a perfectly flat lawn. One little high spot and you scalp.

The Rye Grasses

The two ryes, *Perennial* and *Annual*, are the easiest grasses to grow and are used in the north for quick growth to protect bare ground from rain wash-out. In the south it is the "winter grass." The ryes are strictly one season grasses. They die out in one year and in the south you re-seed every fall.

Redtop

Lawn experts have nothing good to say about *Redtop*, and dismiss it with contempt. Like rye, it is a temporary or "nurse" grass which grows quickly in any soil, wet or dry, sunny or shady. If you are a loner, and care nothing about social status in a mobile home community of lawn freaks, plant Redtop. Even the dogs will pass up your lawn.

The Blue Grasses

There are seven bluegrasses, of which *Kentucky* is probably the best all-around grass in the country. Kentucky bluegrass is not a pure strain but a blend of many on the principle that there is safety in numbers, so it is a mixture of *Newport, Windsor, Merion, Delta* and *Park*. Kentucky bluegrass does not grow well in the shade, but one bluegrass, *Poa Trivialis* grows only in the shade. Of the seven bluegrasses, Merion Kentucky is the most expensive and the most popular with lawn snobs. In suburbia, when station wagon housewives push their baskets up to checkout counters, they always put the big box of Merion Kentucky right on top where us peasants can see it.

SOD IS VALUABLE

If you hate dogs and want to replant with Redtop, don't plow your existing lawn into the ground. It clumps and makes a poor base for the new grass. Sod is a valuable commodity and can be sold. Never destroy sod. Run a two-line ad under miscellaneous in the classifieds. You'll be surprised. A thousand square feet of Merion Kentucky could bring you about $500.

BEWARE OF BARGAIN TOPSOIL

If removing the sod has lowered your lawn's overall surface, you will need to grade it back up again with topsoil. Now here is where you can have some fun with your lawn snob neighbors. Topsoil can be a hellish witch's brew of all diseases and ills known to the science of agronomy. That is why certified topsoil, sometimes called sterilized potting soil, is very expensive and is usually only carried by reputable dealers.

If you want to get even with those snobs, don't buy any of that expensive stuff. Buy that nice looking black stuff from the farmer who has a sign beside his mailbox reading: "All the topsoil you can load for $5."

Lay this "bargain" on your lawn to a depth of about 4 to 6 inches. The experts say 8 to 12 inches, but what do they know? Now seed this with Redtop or Clover, then sit back and wait for the fun. You will see very little grass. The weeds will come up first and take over. You will have no more trouble with dogs. Just with people.

If you live in that subtropical Bermuda grass zone on the map, you are probably retired and spend a lot more time now with the grass than you did back in Detroit. With all the overtime at GM's Cadillac Division, bowling during the winter, and boating on Lake St. Clair during the summer, there was little time for a lawn. Since your own son wanted no part of the lawn either, you just hired kids in the neighborhood to cut it, at least until the first week in July. After that it turned brown and didn't need cutting anymore.

But now in Florida, Arizona, or California there's more time and more good growing weather. There are also more exotic things to grow and bigger lots to grow them on in retirement mobile home communities, most of which do not permit children or pets. So now you can't use dogs as an excuse for not having a nice lawn. You can't say it's a crummy park, nobody bothers with their lawns, so why should you. In Bermuda grass country *everybody* bothers. So you shape up or move back to Detroit.

THE THREE SUBTROPICAL GRASSES

There are three types of lawn cover in the south, the Zoysia grasses, the St. Augustine grasses and, of course, the dominant Bermuda grasses. Once a Zoysia lawn is established, which may take up to three years, it is weed-free, pest-free, drought and wear resistant, easy to maintain and a joy to walk on in your bare feet. Sounds wonderful! But wait. No grass is perfect. The Zoysias have two big faults. It takes so *long* to develop a good lawn (who wants to wait three years?) and they are dormant in winter, producing a heavy brown or straw-colored thatch.

There is only one St. Augustine grass and if you're not too fussy, it makes a fairly attractive and serviceable lawn that is completely insect free. It is a coarse textured grass with very wide blades that is difficult to cut with anything but a good power mower and a sharp blade.

The Dominant Bermuda Grasses

There are eight Bermuda grasses (five of them fairly new hybrids), each supposedly an improvement over all the others. The original three Bermuda strains are *Common, U-3* and *Everglades #3*. Common is the perfect name for the first and original Bermuda grass because in Florida you see it everywhere, in parks, along sidewalks and highways. If well maintained it is practically pest and disease free, which is especially appreciated by all northerners who move south because bluegrasses, which they lived with all their lives, are plagued by disease and insects of all kinds. In the north, you often spend as much time nursing a "sick" lawn as you do cutting it. Disease and insect control are also expensive.

The New Hybrids

One of the new hybrids is *Tifgreen*, very popular right now for home lawns. It is also used all over the south by golf courses for putting greens because it grows very dense, is fine textured and can be cut just as close as you can get with a mower.

Not as good as the above is *T-35-A*, which grows too fast for home use and doesn't take traffic as well. It is good only if you want a fast lawn.

One of the finest textured grass is *Tiffine*. It also has a very unusual yellow-green color, which catches the eye of all northeners the first time they see it. This grass is not recommended if you live in California. In fact, you may not even be able to buy it in that state.

Sunturf is the most unusual grass you will ever see, if you are a northerner heading south to a mobile home. This grass is so fine textured it looks like dark green moss. Cool weather affects its pigmentation and it takes on a striking reddish purple color.

Tifway, last of the Bermudas, has a tendency to grown in crazy whorls. It is a sterile grass, and produces no seeds.But it is also very fine textured, grows very dense and is wear resistant, almost as tough as U-3, which is tough enough for football playing fields.

Dichondra Lawns

There are a few other subtropical grasses not mentioned here, just as there are 1460 other grasses in the general classification, but enough is enough. There is, however, another popular lawn cover in the south Bermuda zone which is not really a grass. It is called the *Dichondra* lawn and is very popular in the milder parts of California and has now spread to the southeastern states. It will grow anywhere in the Bermuda belt on the map and is compatible with Bermuda grass.

The Agricultural Extension Services of some southern states have classified Dichondra as a weed and list it as a member of the bindweed family under the name ponyfoot. It is a ground-hugging plant with broad leaves that are soft and green and it lays close to the ground. A Dichondra lawn sometimes looks like a thick, green shag rug.

California lawns today are a mixture of both Bermuda and Dichondra. The landscaping possibilities with these two are unlimted but since you bought a mobile home originally to get away from grass cutting, I won't go into them. The subject is so vast and complicated it makes do-it-yourself brain surgery look easy.

Planting a Dichondra Lawn

However, if you want a Dichondra lawn, it is no more difficult to have than Bluegrass or Bermuda. You can sow the seed anytime between March 1st and October 15th. Don't sow the seed after October because the ground is too cold for it to germinate and it will just lay there until spring for the birds to feed on. Although the seed germinates fastest in hot weather, mid summer is not a good time to start a Dichondra lawn because there is less rain, and it is difficult to keep the new seedlings moist enough. This is the biggest reason for failures in new plantings. If you start in March, spring rains will keep the seedlings moist, and the lawn will be established enough by mid summer to survive hot, dry weather.

There are two ways to sow a Dichondra lawn. The first way is economical (cheap is more accurate) and calls for 1 ounce of seed per 1000 sq. ft. This will give you a nice Dichondra lawn in about four or five years. The second way is initially much more expensive. It calls for 32 ounces of seed per 1000 sq. ft. This will give you a beautiful lawn in about five weeks.

The first method was recommended by the packagers of the seed when it was first introduced back in the 1950s and Dichondra seed was priced like diamonds. Only movie stars could afford it. The second method is how the pros do it today. Take your choice. One final thing. If, like me, you hate grass cutting, if you are reading this book to *save* money, not blow it on a fancy weed, be warned that Dichondra is *not* a low maintenance lawn cover. It requires the same care, feeding, watering, cutting, and nursing as that Bluegrass lawn you had back in Detroit and hated so fiercely because it interfered with your boating. Dichondra will do the same thing with your boating in St. Petersburg, and it will cost you a bundle that you might better spend on a new spinnaker for your boat.

TREES

The tree, or trees, you will get as part of a package deal when buying a mobile home will be maple, ash, sweet gum, birch, sycamore, black cherry, longleaf pine, elm or crabapple. You will get possibly three small spreading shrubs across the front of your home, with two pyramid yews on the sides. If you're lucky, you might get a small spruce evergreen.

How They are Planted

The mortality rate is very high on these plantings because the work is usually done by teenagers who have never before in their lives planted anything but their feet under a dinner table. I have watched them work. They dig a hole, always too shallow (or too deep). They drop in the ball, pour in a little water, fill the hole, stomp on it a few times, and move on to the next home.

Half of these transplants are dead in three months. The homeowner (who rarely ever sees the work being done) assumes it was done properly. Rarely is the homeowner advised that the new transplants, especially the newly sodded lawn, must be watered regularly for a few weeks or longer. The roots of evergreens should be watered right up to the first frost because they don't shed leaves in the fall and are constantly losing moisture through their needles. New sod must be literally drowned in water every day for at least two weeks or it will die, and when new sod dies it is gone. You roll it up and haul it away to the dump. After your sod has died, the park will come around and tell you that it is your responsibility to haul it away, and your responsibility to replace it.

HOW TO WATER NEW SOD

The best sprinkling system for a newly sodded lawn is the soaker type flat hose with tiny holes which throw a fine misty spray. I had two of these going on my sodded lawn 24 hours a dey for three weeks. I had two other hoses dribbling at the base of my trees and evergreens. All of my plantings survived. Others transplanted on the same day by the same people all died. Nineteen other sodded lawns died for lack of sufficient water. When a newly sodded lawn dies, it is a horrible sight and traumatic experience for the new homeowner. So remember, with new sod you water, water, water and water. Then you move the hose and start all over. A bad transplant job can be saved with proper watering. A good transplant will still die without water.

WHY YOU CAN'T TRANSPLANT WILD TREES

If you are thinking of saving money by making your own transplants, digging up a tree or evergreen somewhere on public land, or the land of a farmer friend, forget it. The transplant will almost certainly die. Trees growing in the wild will have more spread out root systems than nursery stock. A 6-foot maple, for example, will already have roots extending out 10 feet in all directions, whereas that same tree in a nursery will have a compact root system that can easily be dug up and wrapped in a burlap bag that you can lift by yourself. This is because nursery stock is constantly being dug up in various stages of growth and moved. They start out as little 6-inch sprigs planted in rows close together. As they grow, they need more room, so they are moved further apart. This happens many times and is the reason their roots never have a chance to spread out. In digging out a wild tree to a ball size that you can lift without getting a hernia, you will lose 70 to 90 per cent of the roots. With nursery stock you get all the roots, which is the reason they often will give you a money-back guarantee, or replacement.

THE BEST TIME TO BUY

The best time to buy and transplant is in the fall. The best place to buy is direct from a small nursery where the trees are still in the ground. You will get big discounts in October because nurseries always finish up a season with unsold stock that is in the way of transplant rotation.

I bought a 7-foot blue spruce in October for $35. In April that same tree was priced at $100. October is also a good month for transplanting. July is the worst month. The hot sun takes moisture out fast as you soak it down to the roots. Skip one day of watering and all the branches will droop. In October there is less loss of moisture through respiration and the roots in the winter dormant season have an opportunity to adapt easily to their new home. By spring the evergreen, or tree, is settled in its new home and starts to grow.

If you want fast growth, both in trees and evergreens, feed and water. Don't use the same fertilizer that you put on your lawn because trees do not require as much nitrogen. There are special fertilizers available for trees and evergreens.

THE SECRET OF BLUE-GREEN GRASS

Grass thrives on nitrogen. When I asked my green-thumb neighbor why his grass was always a deeper shade of green, almost blue, than mine, he just looked mysterious, the way all lawn freaks do, and gave me some stuff about "iron deficiency" and more feed and water. Well, I was already feeding it and I wasn't buying that bit about "iron." Yet, the color contrast between our two lawns was so striking, I couldn't sleep. Maybe my lawn *did* have tired blood, I thought.

I was determined to find out what my neighbor was using, but I didn't know how. He always fertilized very early in the morning while I was still sleeping. So I did a sneaky thing. I knew where he bought all his lawn stuff. I went there and sought out the owner. "I'm a friend of Steve Kuzcinski," I said. "I want some fertilizer like he uses. He told me what it was, but I forgot."

He went outside, and came back with a large green bag. "I don't sell much of this, so I don't keep it in the store."

The bag contained urea nitrogen, and nothing else. He said, "I presume you know how to use this?"

"Yeah," I lied.

That scared me and I was afraid to use it, and I didn't want to ask *him*. So I checked with a county extension agent and he referred me to an agronomist at Ohio State University who sent me some mimeographed data on "urea-form or urea formaldehyde—nitrogen fertilizers specially compounded and stabilized for slow release."

TYPES OF FERTILIZER

Regular commercial lawn fertilizers that you buy at the hardware store and super market have numbers on the bag like 22-7-12. They represent percentages of nitrogen, phosphorous, potash. But that first number is always nitrogen and the larger the number, the higher the nitrogen content. Sears Roebuck's premium fertilizer has the number 32, which is the highest I have ever seen.

The numbers don't tell you everything because some high nitrogen fertilizers are "quick-acting," some are "slow release." You can tell by just putting some in water. If it dissolves, it is quick-acting. Slow release fertilizers are usually little round pellets in various colors. Put them in water and they just lay there without dissolving.

Non-Burning Fertilizers. Slow dissolving fertilizers are sometimes advertised as "non-burning" and "easy to apply." The "quick acting" will burn if applied just a little too heavily, especially on the overlaps and ends where you stop to turn around and don't close the gate fast enough. When spreading fertilizer, don't let anything distract you. Stop to talk to somebody and you'll forget to close the gate, leaving a pile in one spot. This is what causes "burns," brown spots of dead grass.

Quick-Acting Fertilizers. With all high nitrogen and quick-acting fertilizers, you must water the lawn immediately after, not only to prevent "burning," but to quick release the nitrogen and give your lawn a color change from sickly green to rich blue-green. The right shade of blue-green is an important status symbol in mobile home land. I can drive through a park and just by observing the lawns and grounds, I can compile an in-depth study of the tenants. I may write a book on this some day.

Pure White Urea-Nitrogen. The ultimate status symbol in mobile home land is unadulterated nitrogen in your spreader. It marks you as an aficionado, a True One. Like all members of this cult, you rise at dawn on The Day for the holy ritual of spreading the pure white crystals on dew-wet grass before the sun rises. This is a very delicate ritual and you must not be distracted by anything, which is probably another reason why it is done so early. You can see the tire tracks of your spreader in the wet grass, which is a big help in avoiding those streaks, which can cause you to lose valuable points.

Since pure nitrogen is highly potent, you must use a low spreader setting, usually 2 or 3, and keep moving; never stop for a second. When word gets around among The Others, you will be judged on performance.

I must have passed the test the first time I used pure nitrogen because later when I rode through the park on my 10-speed French racer, I got my first nod of the head from the Right People.

FRUIT TREES: AN ATTRACTIVE NUISANCE

If your trees came as part of a package deal, you probably got stuck with a flowering crabapple or cherry tree (Fig. 8-2). You might even consider digging your tree up, now that you've found it to be an "attractive nuisance."

In an all-adult park, this would not be a problem, but there are few such parks in the north where children are freely admitted. Mobile home parks are fenceless communities where lot lines are not too clearly defined for the comprehension of children. Fruit-bearing trees are a magnet which attract children just as strongly as they attract birds and insects. The fruit is unfit to eat, but it does make wonderful ammunition for bouncing off the roofs of carports, awnings, and homes. The kids will be constantly trespassing on your lawn to gather the fruit. What they leave will rot on your lawn and attract flies. Except for one short week in spring when the blossoms look so pretty, what good is a crabapple tree? It's too small for shade.

Fig. 8-2. Don't ever put in a tree like this. In any park which accepts children, fruit bearing trees are an attractive nuisance which bring nothing but grief. Kids will be constantly trespassing over your lawn to pick the fruit. Then, because it is unfit to eat, they will throw it on other homes, up on roofs, and at passing cars.

FAST GROWING SHADE TREES

Because of a mobile home's natural propensity for absorbing heat from the sun, big shade trees are highly desirable, and you don't want to wait 50 years to grow one. The fastest growing trees are the various elms, like the *Moline Elm*, the *Chinese Elm*, and the *American Elm*. They will reach a height of 30 feet in ten years, 15 feet in five years, which is high enough for shade beside a mobile home. They eventually will grow to 50 and 80 feet.

Other fast growers reaching the same heights are the *Norway* and *Silver Maple*, and the *Moraine Locust*. These trees are deciduous. That means they shed their leaves in the fall. This is something to consider because the maples can literally bury a mobile home under leaves and you have all those plastic bags to line up in front of your home for the garbage collectors. Will they take all those extra bags? If not, you might consider two other large shade trees, evergreen types, which do not shed their leaves, the *Coast Live Oak* and the *Holly Oak*.

Smaller trees, which grow to about 30 feet and are used as wind and privacy screens, are actually more suitable around a mobile home. There are five such trees which do not shed their leaves, the *Glossy Privet*, the *Pittosporum*, the *Silver Dollar Gum*, the *Buckthorn*, and the *Incense Cedar*. There are hundreds more, with crazy names you never heard of, and if the above are not available in your section of the country, the nurseryman can recommend something else with the same characteristics. Remember, you want fast growth, 15 feet in five years, and you want no leaves to stuff in plastic bags.

THE IDEAL MOBILE HOME TREES

If you seek the advice of an expert, he will tell you that the maples are too large and too greedy for moisture and food. The elms are too delicate and disease prone. In large fast growing trees your choice is limited. Variety increases as you go down in size, and no matter where you live, you will have an unlimited choice in trees which top at 15 to 30 feet. This is the ideal mobile home size, and, in the non-leaf shedding type, will create a minimum of litter. If you have a corner lot, a row of incense cedar is a thing of beauty, in addition to being a privacy and wind screen.

HOW TO PLANT A TREE

Trees should be transplanted *only* while dormant, in autumn or spring. In the fall get that burlap ball in the ground at least four weeks before soil freeze-up, and dribble water on it one hour every day until the first freeze.

In spring, plant immediately after the ground thaws. Never, *never* leave roots exposed to the sun, not even for that short period while you are digging the hole. Dribble some water from a hose over the ball while you are working. If you must, for unavoidable reasons, delay planting, put the ball in a temporary shallow hole, cover with soil, and keep moist. In nursery jargon, this is called "heeling in."

Dig the hole a foot wider than the ball, and just deep enough so that when you fill it in, you will just barely cover the burlap on top—no deeper! If you want fast growth (and you do), backfill your hole with topsoil rather than dirt. All nurseries sell a special compost material for this very purpose. You put in a 4-inch layer of this compost in the bottom of the hole. The ball goes on top of this. You spray with water, then a layer of topsoil, more water, another layer of compost, water, more topsoil. You keep doing this in layers until the hole is filled. As each layer is applied, tamp the fill with a length of 2 × 4.

If you use good compost from the nursery, and you plant in spring, fertilizing is unnecessary. If you don't use compost, sprinkle some 10-10-10 fertilizer with the topsoil.

Regarding that burlap which encloses the roots, it is not necessary to do anything with it. One group of experts suggest cutting the bindings after it is in the hole and peeling the burlap back away from the trunk. Another group of experts suggest leaving the burlap alone, that it decays rapidly and in no way interferes with root growth. Take your choice.

SHRUBS

Shrubs are very desirable on the mobile home scene because they break up the severity of all that aluminum. Homes on corner lots sometimes look sharp and boxy—and corners are a good spot for the erect form of shrubs with vertical lines like the *Althea, Highbush Cranberry* and *French Lilac* which reach heights of 10 and 12 feet. They not only will hide your downspouting, but be well watered at the same time.

Some shrubs can withstand severe pruning better than others. These are the type that you see pruned with flat tops and sides, so often used to define lot lines in place of a fence. The *Japanese Barberry, Alpine Currant* and *Amur River Privet* are the small shrubs which grow from 2 to 6 feet. The *Japanese Holly, Chinese Elm* and *Boxwood* will reach heights of 10 and 12 feet.

Mobile home skirting, although practical and useful, is esthetically satisfying only to a ground mole. It is always being damaged by wind, playing children and lawnmower tires, which leave dent and black marks. A row of shrubs, hiding the skirting, is so much nicer to look at —and there's a bonus, too, if you live in areas of severe winters. Only men who work the seas or the western plain states appreciate and understand the power of wind.

The old *Life* magazine once printed a memorable photograph showing what wind can do. In the kitchen of a plains home stood a pyramid pile of snow five feet high. All the doors and windows were closed tight. Where did the snow come from? The wind had blown it in through the keyhole. *That* is what wind can do.

The spreading *Japanese Quince* and the *Rock Spray Cotoneaster*, which grow to a height of three feet, are ideal for planting along the skirting. Just don't plant them too close together because they grow laterally as well as up. At a height of three feet, they will just cover your skirting, be easy to prune and make an excellent windbreak. Stay away from rounded arching shrubs because they will grow to heights of ten feet and reach your roof level if not pruned regularly.

LAWN MOWERS

In the short time that I hve lived in a mobile home, I have owned seven lawnmowers, and I *still* haven't found one that I like. Everybody thinks I'm a dummy because I'm always buying lawnmowers. Maybe I am, or maybe the grass war has changed me. What was once a simple chore is now a career. I may write a book about grass and what it does to people.

I have just purchased my eighth lawnmower, a manual hand-operated reel mower that cost almost $100 (with grass catcher). Wanda is threatening to have me committed because I am now currently using three mowers. There is a reason.

I have an electric which I use only for thatching purposes. I have it equipped with one of those special thatch removing blades. Why electric? This particular mower has one of those new type electric motors that stops instantly when switched off. This is something new in power tools now and very desirable, too. When you finish cutting with a hand power saw, you don't have to wait five minutes for the blade to stop spinning.

In thatching (power raking is another term) it is absolutely essential that you keep moving and be able to stop the blade instantly when you come to an area where you must turn. Stop moving just for a second and the thatch blade will tear up the lawn. The instructions that come with thatch conversion kits for rotary mowers warn you of this, but they don't tell you how to handle this problem. This is the reason I bought the new electric with instant stop motor. It works very well as a converted power rake. Of course, you can rent regular power rakes, and I almost did until I figured the cost. Unless the savings is substantial, I don't like to rent.

Electric Mowers

Shortly after moving into my mobile home, when I found out the park would ruin your lawn if they cut it, I bought my first electric. We were instantly incompatible and I hated it. That 100 feet of electric cord was a constant irritation. My neighbor uses electric and loves it. He flips that cord around like a professional dryfly caster and it lays down exactly where he wants it. If you can learn to live with the cord, the electric mowers are ideally suited for the bluegrass country mobile homer who lives on a regular size lot. Corner lots can sometimes be quite large, often with two and three times as much lawn area as the regular lots. But even with the extra grass to cut, the electrics are still desirable because of noise pollution factor in a crowded community. There is no gas or oil to fool with. To clean, you just turn the mower upside down and no gas or dirty oil will leak out on the sidewalk.

The Two Cycles

All my life I have had a love affair with 2-cycle engines, mainly because of outboard motors. The smell of 2-cycle fumes affects me. The happiest days of my life have been spent at the stern of a rented boat fussing with a motor that wouldn't start. In my tackle box, along with the artificial lures, there were always spare spark plugs and copper washers. There were times when I thought the spark plug might catch more fish then the artificial lures.

The 2-cycle engine is one of the simplest functioning systems ever invented by man. It has only three moving parts, (a piston, a connecting rod, and a crank shaft), which is the reason they can be made incredibly small. I have one that runs a 120-volt generator delivering 500 watts, and you can hold it in the palm of your hand.

The Four Cycles

The 4-cycle engine, (which is what you have in your automobile) must have valves for exhaust and intake, and a camshaft and timing gears to open the valves at the right time. It must also have a crankcase for oil storage. The 2-cycle is lubricated by oil which is mixed with the gas. This gas/oil mixture enters the engine by way of the crankshaft housing and passes up through a slot in the cylinder wall into the combustion chamber. The gasoline vaporized, burns, and is exhausted out through another slot on the opposite side. The oil does not burn or vaporize, but remains behind to lubricate. Very simple and efficient.

But when this wonderful little power plant is put into a lawnmower or snow blower, something gets lost. I have—or had—a famous brand name 2-cycle snow blower that just would not start in cold weather, which is the only time it snows. I have—or had—a 2-cycle Big Name lawnmower that would not start in warm weather, which is the only time grass grows. When I finally did get these beasts started, I was too tired to blow snow or cut grass. And yet, I am something of an expert around 2-cycle engines. These engines are definitely not for little old ladies and retired ribbon clerks who can't change a light bulb. There has to be a reason why so few manufacturers use the 2-cycle on their lawnmowers. Offhand, I only know of one Big Name manufacturer who does. I know of hundreds who use the 4-cycle, which is bigger, heavier, and more expensive to build. I will always love those little cussed 2-cycles, but I will never again own one in anything but a chain saw or outboard motor with self starter.

The Best 4-Cycle Mowers

In 4-cycle mowers, you have an endless variety—rotary, reel, manual and self-propelled. There are also riding mowers, but these you don't need. The self-propelled rotary is useful mainly in blue-grass country, and if you have a large lot and few trees to work around. The constant maneuvering around shrubs, and trees can be tiring with a self-propelled that has power on the rear wheels. You wear yourself out engaging and disengaging the power as you work around the obstacle course in a well landscaped lawn. If you must have self-propelled, at least get one with power on the front wheels. With this type it isn't necessary to disengage the clutch each time you stop. You just raise the front wheels, back up, and maneuver on the rear wheels.

The Best Manuals

The manual push type rotary (with the spinning cutting blade) is the most popular of all mowers and the cheapest to own, starting at around $50. Only with a rotary can you cut tall grass and weeds (Fig. 8-3) and it is here where the self-propelled is useful and worth the price.

In a manual rotary, you want something light, preferably in magnesium which is much lighter than aluminum, and in the 18-inch cut. A 22-inch cut on a small lawn doesn't make much difference in cutting time, but it does make a big difference in weight to push around. Easy cutting height adjustment is very important because with bluegrass you must change cutting heights as hot, dry weather approaches. In April you start with 1½-inch cut, gradually going up until by mid July you're cutting at 3-inches. If you don't do this, you'll have nothing but thatch by the 4th of July.

Grass Clippings

There are differences of opinion amoung experts on the impor-tance of catching the grass clippings in a mower bag. or letting them lay. Grass clippings can be a big disposal problem in some parks where you are limited to a specific number of bags you can leave for garbage pick-up. Also, if your neighbor does and you don't, you must be so careful that your mower doesn't exhaust clippings on *his* lawn. To grass catch or not to grass catch is a personal decision you

Fig. 8-3. For cutting tall grass and weeds, the power driven rotary is the best of all mowers. However, it is almost useless for fine Bermuda lawns which look good only when cut short (½ inch or less). On Bermudas, your best mower is a reel type with up to 12 cutting blades, as used by professional gardeners or golf course groundskeepers.

must make. It is not a big deal either way unless you are a grass snob and don't want to lose class.

The New Mowers

Recently a new mower came on the market with the bag directly *behind* the machine and between the handles, and it's a big bag, too, holding about three bushels. I am a helpless idiot around anything labeled "new." Wanda hates for me to go grocery shopping with her. If I see anything marked "new," I automatically drop it in the basket. So I bought the "new" lawnmower.

The grass catcher on this mower is the best on the market, but the machine itself is a wearisome beast to work with because it has power drive on the rear wheels, and a crazy Rube Goldberg friction type clutch device that never completely disengages. This makes the machine very hard to push around shrubs and trees. Each time you empty the bag, you must stop the engine or get hit in the face with a blast of air out of the discharge chute.

Another Big Name manufacturer has also come out with a competitive bag-in-the-rear mower, and minor improvements, like a shut-off flap in the discharge chute to protect you from that blast of air. This mower has power on the front wheels, but when that big grass bag in the rear is filled, the weight lifts the front wheels off the ground and you have no traction. At this writing, Sears Roebuck also has a new bag-in-the-rear mower. But, as I remarked earlier, I have yet to find a mower that I really like. Every mower is a compromise.

Self-Starting Mowers

Are you intrigued by those self-starting mowers where you just turn a key? I was, too, and I bought one. It took just three grass cuttings to learn that the small battery pack 12-volt motor was a boy sent to do a man's job. This little motor quickly developed high resistance at the brushes and armature. The least little dirt film on that armature, the voltage dropped and there just wasn't enough reserve amperage in a battery pack. The starter just groaned, like the battery was dead, yet it had been on charge the previous 24 hours. I cleaned the armature and it immediately cranked with new vigor. It worked fine for three more grass cuttings, and again the armature had to be cleaned. This went on all summer. I finally gave the mower away. The new owner now won't speak to me.

Why doesn't this problem occur in automobile starters? Because there is enough reserve amperage in an auto battery to overcome resistance. The lead-acid battery is able to deliver 300-500 amps to a DC motor which has heavy windings to handle such a load. If you ever accidently caused a short across the hot side of your car battery with a screwdriver, you saw what happened to your tool after a scary display of sparks. In a split second you can burn off the end of a screwdriver or melt a strand of 18-gauge wire. You just don't get that kind of energy in a dry lawnmower battery pack, which is nothing more than re-chargeable nickle-cadmium flashlight batteries. Lead-acid batteries are made in small sizes for motorcycles, some no larger then a quart carton of milk. They could be even made smaller for lawnmowers. So why do they send a boy to do a man's job?

The Reel Mowers

The rotary mower is unsuited for Bermuda grasses, which must be cut so much shorter to look right. Burmuda cut at a 2-inch height looks horrible, and quickly turns to thatch. Getting down to 1-inch with a rotary is risky, unless a lawn is absolutely flat. The slightest hump will be scalped, and you can't get that smooth putting green look with a rotary. For quality and appearance, nothing beats the old reel mowers, and for a 1/2-inch cut, you *must* use handpower. Although powered reel mowers do not scalp as readily as rotaries, they will on an uneven surface. The hand-powered reels give you warning when you come to high spots because they suddenly get hard to push or just stop when you hit a bump. With power you keep right on going and slice off the humps or high spots.

The better reel mowers have five blades. Economy versions have only four. Golf course putting green reel mowers have up to 12 blades. Professional gardeners, who work on Bermuda lawns, use a special type of rotary with six or seven blades. These special mowers are available on special order to any homeowner who doesn't mind paying the price and who wants the ultimate in quality on his Bermuda lawn. In bluegrass country you have to look hard to find a reel mower of any kind late in the season, and by July you have to special order a manual reel out of the Sears or Ward's catalogs.

The Dangerous Rotaries

The popular rotary is also the most dangerous piece of machinery in the American garage, next to the automobile. My dentist lost his big toe to one last summer. He gave the mower to his father-in-law, who proceeded to lose the same toe the first time

Fig. 8-4. The rotary is also the most dangerous of all mowers, accounting for thousands of lost fingers and toes every year.

he used the mower. In a neighboring park, a young woman who had just finished cutting the grass raised the front end to remove those clumps of grass which build up if you don't use a grass catcher. The cutting blade was in the way, so she moved it with her hand. The engine, still hot, kicked over. She lost four fingers.

This happens so many times with women and children because they don't understand that turning that cutting blade is the same as pulling the starter cord. Even men, who know better, will forget and turn that blade with their hand while the engine is hot. Another thoughtless act is often committed when the mower cutting height is changed. Without bothering to shut off the engine, a boy will lift up one side of the mower housing to change the cutting height, not realizing that the cutting blade is very close to the edge. Lost fingertips are the result (Fig. 8-4).

Power driven reel mowers are considerably less dangerous in this respect because the cutting blades turn *only* when in gear and moving. A rotary blade never stops turning until the engine is stopped. Most injuries occur while a mower is standing still, with the engine still running or idling.

The Best Mower for Bermuda Grass

For Bermuda grass, the best and safest mower is a manual reel, preferably with five or more cutting blades. Let the professionals use those special seven blade rotaries. Mobile home lawns are small. If you cut to the recommended 1/2-inch height, and often, you don't have to catch the cuttings, and the physical effort of pushing will be good exercise (and, for your wife, far cheaper then joining Vic Tanny for figure control). It is only when you delay, or miss a cutting, that the lawn must be raked. Too much dead grass left on the lawn is not only unsightly, but cuts off oxygen to the grass and builds up a mat which interferes with water and food penetration. As the experts say, "A little is good for your lawn, too much is bad."

Although the manual reel mowers will do a superior job on cool season grass, you will rarely see one in bluegrass country. There are only two in my park, and I have one. But there are over 400 rotaries. That figures out at 200 to 1, if you like statistics. And according to statistics, 2 out of every 5 mobile homeowners are expected to buy a new lawn mower this year.

Save When You Move— The Right Way

9

If the decision to move is forced on you, don't panic. When you first get that registered letter from some law firm coldly stating in legalese that your lease has been terminated and you must remove your mobile home from such and such premises within 30 days, you will imagine the worst. Typically, you will have visions of rough-looking men showing up on the 30th day in trucks and tractors, kicking on your doors, yelling that your water, gas, electric, telephone are being disconnected and not to use the toilets.

Stop worrying. I have seen dozens of evictions and it isn't like that at all. Remember, it costs money to move a mobile home ten inches. If management takes on the sticky responsibility of moving your home without your consent, they open up a can of worms. Many things can happen. If little children are involved, if the mother comes down sick, there will be bad publicity. This will attract contingency-fee lawyers which, in turn, will bring more bad publicity and court orders and temporary injunctions.

The entire mobile home industry, and their national and state associations, all shrink in horror from anything that might bring bad press. The reason: it immediately affects sales and business in general. This is a vulnerable industry with image (and other) problems.

The "rules and regulations" by which all parks maintain order and discipline are their Achille's heel. Constitutional issues are involved. Just because no court test of these issues has ever been made doesn't mean they *won't* be.

Some federal judge once said, "No American should expect to automatically get his constitutional rights just because they are there. You still have to fight for them again and again, every day of your life."

Under the law, any citizen can challenge any law or restraint on his liberty and put it to a court test. While his challenge awaits a final decision of the courts, he cannot be arrested, restrained or penalized in any way. A federal judge will issue an indefinite stay against the execution of any order against the petitioner.

Someday, somewhere a mobile homer is going to get mad, put up a TV antenna on the roof of his home and say to park management, "Let the courts decide if I take it down."

And that TV antenna is going to *stay* on the roof of that mobile home for years until the U.S. Supreme Court decides the constitutional issues of whether a man's home is his castle, even if it is on rented land.

This is the reason why you will not be evicted for getting into a big argument with the manager about that carport extension you put up yourself without asking his permission, or that red barn utility building you bought and erected yourself. Of course, it's all wood and all the others in the park are steel. He may even try to scare you with one of those registered letters from a law firm.

Just remember, they never evict *anyone* for rule infractions regardless of what you may hear. Yes, yes, you personally know of a friend who was evicted for breaking some rule, but that's only what your friend *told* everybody. In every one of these cases, the real truth is eviction was for non-payment of rent and *that* is solid legal grounds for eviction. If you want to break park rules, okay, but don't you *ever* miss one rent payment.

I personally know people who, through no fault of their own, are out of work and have fallen six and eight months behind on their rent. Yet, they haven't even been threatened with eviction. Park managements can be very tolerant with what they call "good tenants," but with persistent troublemakers they just sit back and wait for a solid legal excuse, and out you go.

Another solid legal excuse for eviction is breaking the law—any law, even minor misdemeanors. This and non-payment of rent are the two main reasons behind *all* evictions regardless of what evicted people say for appearances sake. For example, your kid is picked up by county sheriffs for breaking some windows in a display model home. The legal term for this is vandalism. Of course, your kid didn't really throw the stone, but he was with some other boys who did. Only *your* boy was recognized and picked up.

Your son has character and will not rat on the others. He takes the rap all by himself. You have to appear in juvenile court and are ordered to pay for the damages. Although juvenile court proceedings and records are sealed from the public, and technically there is no way of proving that your son broke any law, the fact still remains that *you* were ordered by a juvenile judge to pay for the damages. And this is where you get it in the end for insulting the manager because he kept sending you those warning notes for parking your car in the street overnight. You shouldn't have called him a jerk, even if it is true.

Like I said, you can get away with breaking park rules and insulting managers, but don't you *ever* miss a rent payment or get cited for speeding in the park.

HOW TO MOVE IN 30 DAYS

So now you have 30 days in which to move and your wife is no help because all she does is moan and bawl. So what do you do?

While your wife is crying herself out, get on the phone and call all the other parks in your area. Don't be concerned or fearful that you might be blacklisted because of the eviction. On the contrary, you will be welcomed unless you try to get into one of those super-parks that is for adults only. There are very few parks outside of Florida and California that are filled. They all have big mortgages and even a 10 percent vacancy hurts. They're all crying for more aluminum and warm bodies—even aluminum and bodies kicked out of other parks. So don't be fooled when the manager puts on an act about doing you a big favor in letting you move into his aluminum concentration camp. The owners have a blowtorch aimed at him to get cracking and fill those lots.

Moving Out of Town

If you are moving to another town, or another state, you will need *Woodall's Mobile Home & Park Directory*, previously mentioned, and available in any book store for $5.95. You can telephone or write to parks in the city you are moving to, but make a personal visit before you select a lot.

Your next important step is to select a mover. You will find all these companies listed in Woodall's. These are big organizations who operate nationally, and their sole business is the moving of mobile homes all over the United States, or just across town to another park. Listed under each company will be names of states where they have terminal offices, and a list of the cities in those states.

If you live in a large city, there will almost certainly be a terminal office of one of these companies listed in the Yellow Pages under "Mobile Homes—Transporting." If they don't have an office in the town nearest your park, they will still be listed in the Yellow Pages with a toll-free number to call. If by chance you cannot find such a listing, go through Woodall's until you find a transport company with terminals in your state. Telephone (collect) the terminal or district office nearest you and they will give you a free moving estimate.

These big companies all operate under special license of the Interstate Commerce Commission and if you are moving across the state, or to another state, they will help you obtain the necessary permits for each state that you pass through. Their personnel will also help you with packing and getting your undercarriage ready for travel.

Most of the transporters of mobile homes in interstate traffic are members of the Mobile Housing Carriers Conference and charge a uniform rate. They also have minimum rate charges for short hauls, like to another park in your area.

Beware of Small Local Movers

Moving charges are based on the length and width of your home. Beware of small local outfits who offer you a "deal." When your home is delivered, they hit you with all sorts of hidden charges, like flagging service, lowboy and I.C.C. lights, and special expenses for mechanical and spring trouble or tire blowouts.

Certified carriers are required by the federal government, and various states, to file evidence that they carry adequate insurance to protect your home in transit. If you use a non-regulated carrier, you alone are responsible and liable for damage suits if anyone gets hurt. You could lose your home. You could be cited by the I.C.C. for "aiding and abetting an illegal operation."

The Complex Laws

Each state has its own complex laws governing the transporting of mobile homes. This is another reason why you should deal only with professionals who do business in all the states and *know* the laws.

The moving of a mobile home, even from one park to another in the same city, can be very expensive. You can save money, but not by moving the home itself. Leave that to the professionals.

HOW TO SAVE IN MOVING

You save big money by doing all the preparatory work. This is very time-consuming and builds up fantastic labor charges. For example, all your awnings must come down. The carport must come down and that enclosed porch which cost you a bundle and you never use (Fig. 9-1). Every piece must be carefully marked so that it goes back up again the same way. The skirting must be removed and marked the same way. Some of the screws can be re-used, but most will be too rusty, especially all the exposed screws in the carport. Do *not* throw any rusty fastenings away. Store them in coffee jars. This will give you an accurate count later on how many to buy as replacements. Stainless steel screws are expensive and you should buy only what you need.

Your steel utility building, if more than a year old, will be rusty and hardly worth disassembling. Give it to somebody. When you replace it later, take a long look at aluminum utility buildings. They cost a little more but in the long run will save you money.

Don't Haul Freight in Your Home

Heed this warning! *Don't* try to "save money" by hauling all the above inside your home. Mobile homes were not designed or built to haul freight!

Just recently a tenant in my park moved his home to Mississippi. I watched him for two weeks doing all the preparatory work himself and he did it well. Everything was carefully catalogued and stacked in the driveway. A week before the transport tractor was due, he and his wife moved in with friends.

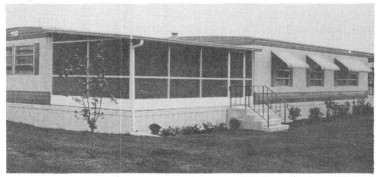

Fig. 9-1. Nothing in life is permanent, but we mobile homers never think of this when we add on the porch enclosures, awnings, and fully enclosed carports. These are the things that build up astronomical moving costs—they must all be slowly and laboriously disassembled, packed, and transported, and later reassembled.

189

The electricity, gas, water, telephone, and sewage were disconnected. I was amazed, watching that skinny little old man in his late sixties jack up that 70-foot mobile home and put on those eight tires all by himself. I thought sure he would ask my help with the hitch (Fig. 9-2), which is quite heavy. With his wife helping, he just inched it up gradually on cement blocks until it was in position to be bolted back in its original position on the frame.

Up to this point he had done an excellent job and saved himself about two thousand dollars on this end of the move. I had nothing but admiration for this retired high school English teacher who had never before in his life done anything more physical than wind his watch. Then, three days before the transport company tractor was due, he blew it. He was headed for disaster and I couldn't stop him.

All the material piled up high in the driveway—the carport, the awnings, the skirting, the utility building, the air conditioner—*everything* was loaded into the home as if it was a railroad freight car. When I saw him starting to load the heavy cement blocks also in his home, I had to butt in. He just brushed off my concern.

"These Holly Parks are built like a tank,"

"But not the *tires!*" I said.

"These are 12 ply tires and cost over 100 bucks each," he said. "They're designed for heavy loads."

Further discussion on the subject was useless, so I left him with his loading labors. He eventually had the interior of that home so jammed that he had to walk over things to get from one room to another, and often bumped his head on the ceiling.

The transport companies have preparation manuals which they will provide you on request. One of the first things they warn against is overloading. Mechanical troubles, tire blowouts— *anything* which causes delay—are at the owner's expense and payable on arrival of your home by cash or certified check. They will not accept a personal check.

Your Springs and Tires

Your tires and springs are a good visual loading gauge. There must be a 3-inch clearance between the tops of your tires and the floor to allow for free movement without rubbing. Your springs must have a proper arc. If they are straight, you are overloaded! Remember, transport companies, according to tariff regulations, are not liable for failure of tires, axles, springs, wheels, frames, or other mechanical components.

Fig. 9-2. Modern parks today do not permit hitches like this to be visible. They are removed and usually hidden under the home, where they rust badly. The transport driver will not move an inch if he is dissatisfied with how you put this hitch back on, especially if a bolt is missing. This happens often because the bolts are just left lying on the ground and children pick them up to play with.

Five days after the home was pulled out of the park, I got a long distance phone call from Mississippi. The home had not arrived. When did it leave?

Two days later I got another phone call. There had been a breakdown just outside Covington, Kentucky. A broken spring, a flat tire. The driver had said he could never make it unless the load was lightened.

A large truck had to be rented in Mississippi, driven up to a small town in Kentucky where repairs were being made, then loaded. This caused a delay of five days, which were added to the moving charges. The driver is paid while waiting. He has to be fed and lodged. He is paid for helping to unload the home. He is paid for re-arranging and re-packing things in the home, which should have been done right in the first place. The end result was that the schoolteacher paid out an additional $1500 for his move to Mississippi.

This is *not* the way to save money.

HOW TO HANDLE HEAVY STUFF

The proper way would have been to rent a large U-Drive-It truck and loaded *it* with all the heavy stuff and freight. They have U-Drive-It trucks that are equipped with hydraulic lifts. You can also rent hand-trucks for easy one man handling of heavy things like refrigerators and air conditioners. The rental on this would have been small compared to the $1500 that was not "saved" by cutting corners and almost losing the home.

PREPARATION

There is more to moving a mobile home than just hitching it up to a commercial transport tractor. There can be weeks of preparation, and this is what builds up the costs. There are high labor charges for two men to take down your awning, your carport, your enclosed porch (Fig. 9-1), your utility building, and so on. You can reduce what could be a $3000 move down to $500 by doing all the preparatory work yourself, but only if you do it right.

Things You Must Supply

Regardless of who does the actual inside preparatory work, *you* (the shipper) must provide all the necessary packing and blocking materials, such as:

☐ Cardboard boxes for all breakable items such as dishes, loose objects, etc.

☐ Plentiful supply of newspapers for packing and padding purposes.

☐ A supply of 1½ inch masking tape for securing things like fixtures, drawers, mirrors, and windows.

☐ Heavy twine and small rope for tying many things down.

As a mobile home moves over the road, vibrations cause everything to shift forward. Soon everything in each room is piled up against a forward wall, causing damage. You prepare for this by moving all padded furniture and chairs flush up against a forward wall where they can't go anywhere. In the kitchen, the table is turned upside down over newspapers on the floor, then pushed up against a forward wall and padded. The kitchen chairs are stacked over the inverted table, taped or tied to the legs, and padded to prevent chafing.

Weight to the rear of the wheels should be kept to a minimum. All heavy items should be forward of the wheels. This puts some of the load on the towing tractor, which has the necessary springs to handle this.

All mirrors on doors and medicine cabinets should be taped over their entire length to prevent vibration and cracking. Large windows, also vulnerable to vibration, should be taped in the same way. All small windows should be cranked in the closed position.

Remove everything from the top shelves in clothes closets and kitchen closets. Bottom shelves need not be emptied, but they should be packed with paper stuffing to prevent movement. Clothes should be removed from closets and used as padding. If left hanging on the rods, vibration will cause them to break away from the wall.

The Cumulative Effect of Vibration

The longer the road travel, the more damaging vibration can be because its effect is cumulative. Don't take any chances with anything that is loose, or can be torn loose. This especially applies to standing floor lamps, table lamps and their shades, mounted wall lights, and their glass fixtures. If hanging fixtures cannot be taken down, the bulbs and glass should be removed and the fixture tied to some solid object to prevent swinging.

Plants should be packed in large carton boxes with paper stuffing around the pots to keep them from tipping. Beds and chests of drawers in these rooms should be moved to a forward wall. Do not put heavy items on beds because the springs cause a bouncing action. Incidentally, the beds are a good place to stack clothing taken down from closets.

Drawers. All drawers which face either to the front or the back of the home must be firmly secured by partially driving a thin finishing nail through the sides. Start with the bottom drawer, pulling it out about eight inches, and working up. Many manufacturers do this when shipping homes and you can use the same holes. Remember, drawers can do funny things, which is how haunted houses sometimes get their reputation.

Drawers on each side of the home need not be nailed. Taping will hold them in the closed position. Contents of drawers need not be removed, unless they are so heavy that movement could break the securing tape or nail. Just pack the drawers with stuffing to prevent movement.

Doors. On anything that moves, doors can be a problem. If they move and squeak in stationary haunted homes, imagine what they do in moving homes. All folding doors and sliding doors in closets must be taped. Hinge doors between rooms can be secured by two small blocks of wood driven into the floor on each side of the partially opened door with long, thin finishing nails. Don't worry about that hole through the rug. You'll never see it.

Plumbing. If your home is moving from or into a cold climate, the plumbing will have to be protected. When the cold water line is disconnected, flush the toilets. Prepare a mixture of 50 percent water and anti-freeze, pour this into the toilet tanks, and flush again. This will take care of the traps. Pour some of this same mixture down all wash basins, kitchen sinks and bathtub drains. The bathtub can now be used for storage—after being lined with blankets.

When the main water line is broken under your home, water in the pipes will succumb to the force of gravity, and slowly dribble out under your home. The transport companies suggest that the lines be blown out with compressed air, but don't worry about that tiny amount of water that might remain in the pipes. It is only when pipes are filled with water that they cause damage because there is no room left for expansion. However, if you are the worrying type, and don't own a compressor, I will tell you what another friend did when he moved his home to the Upper Peninsula of Michigan last January, where it often gets colder than Alaska.

Instead of using expensive anti-freeze, my friend bought 25 pounds of sodium chloride, that stuff cities in the north put on their streets to melt snow and rust cars. It is also called rock salt. He mixed a briny solution, poured a bucketful into his toilet tanks, and flushed it down through the traps. Then he filled the tanks full a second time, opened the inlet water lines, and let the salt brine drain back into the water lines and dribble out under the home on the ground.

Salt lowers the freezing point of water. If it ever does freeze, it's soft and mushy. The small amount of salt brine in the pipes will quickly flush out when water service is restored.

Bracing Large Appliances. When your mobile home was originally shipped from the factory, the automatic washer, dryer, and refrigerator all had special braces outside and inside. You probably threw them away. Now you must improvise. You can use strips of 2-inch aluminum duct tape on your dryer drum and washer tumbler. Tape the doors shut.

The compressor on your refrigerator is suspended on springs and will bounce around constantly. On a long move it could be damaged. Use a block of wood to raise it up just enough to take it off free suspension. Also, be sure the refrigerator is secured to the floor. Refrigerators have a nasty way of tipping over if they face towards the front and the driver must brake suddenly, which happens at least once on every long haul (transport drivers say). You will almost certainly find that your refrigerator is secured somewhere, if not on the floor, then bracket-secured to the wall in back to keep it from falling forward on sudden emergency stops.

If your laundry equipment is in a bathroom closet, dryer stacked on top of the washer, they had better be well fastened down. Brace the blanket-padded closet door against the washer-dryer with a 2 × 4 so it can't swing open. If the washer and dryer are in a utility room, lag screw them to the floor.

Hot Water Tank. Drain the hot water tank. Remove the draft hood on top because it will only fall off. The plumbing connections, top and bottom, are usually sufficient to hold down the tank, but check to be sure if your move is a long one because funny things start to happen after that first 100 miles of bouncing and vibration. Things start to come loose that you never knew existed and you'll find little parts laying on the floor and you may never find out what they came from.

Sewer Pipe. When the messy and smelly sewer lines are disconnected, stuff the open ends with paper and ship them in the U-Drive-It truck along with all the other dismantled appurtenances. This is one more reason why you must rent a truck. Do you want that stinking pipe in your home? And what about your three concrete entrance steps? They weigh a half-ton each. With a hydraulic lift truck, you can manage.

Record Players. Be especially careful with the tone arm on a hi-fi or a record player. Tie it to the arm rest with heavy rubber bands. Console TVs can be layed screen down on the floor, braced with carton boxes. The same with portables, always face down so nothing can ram through the screen.

Remove window-type air conditioners and ship them in the truck because they are very heavy and messy. If you have a roof type water cooler, it will have to be drained and taken down. The same with under-the-floor mounted central air conditioners because they hang lower than the axle and are in a vulnerable position to be road damaged. Insurance underwriters would reject any damage claims.

Furnaces. With a gas furnace, you just turn off the pilot and main gas supply. With LP fuel, you must turn off the furnace at least two hours ahead of time to allow fuel in the furnace to be consumed. Fuel storage tanks on heaters are a fire hazard and must be drained.

ITEMS NOT TRANSPORTABLE

Transport companies will not move a home that has anything alive inside, such as birds or animals of any kind, including goldfish. Some states do not permit plants or vegetation to cross their borders. Here again is where that U-Drive-It pays for itself. All your wife's plants, the evergreens you dug up, your motorbike, bicycles, your son's motor scooter, the lawn mower, garden tools, oil drums, and all your tool boxes (Fig. 9-3) go in the truck.

INSURANCE COVERAGE

Only your basic home and the factory installed equipment is covered by the transport companies' insurance. Your personal property is covered at a reduced rate, or valuation. If you want more coverage on personal property, it can be arranged after you declare total value and pay the extra premiums.

UNDERCARRIAGE CHECKS

You, the shipper, are responsible for the structural capacity and mechanical ability of your mobile home to survive a move, short or long, so you had better be sure it can. Transport companies say that overloaded tires are the biggest cause of trouble in moving a home. An overlooked cause for some of these failures is tire deterioration. Tires are often stored on the ground under a home for years. If your tires have been stored in this manner for a year or more, don't gamble. Trade them in for new ones if your move is a long one. This may not sound like a money-saving idea, but it is when you sell the tires later. Why let all that money deteriorate under your home? You can always buy new ones again when you move.

If tires can deteriorate, so can mechanical gear. Remove the axle dust caps on the wheels and re-pack with new grease. Burned out wheel bearings are another frequent cause for expensive delays and repairs. The transport driver will check all your wheels (especially the lugs) for tightness. If any are missing (as so often happens because they are left on the ground) he won't travel until they are replaced. You will be wasting valuable time running around to buy new ones. The driver will also check the hitch and lights. And be sure you have a current license in your name prominently displayed because some states will impound your home for this violation.

All the above chores have to be done by *somebody*. You can save hundreds or thousands if you do them yourself. However, we are getting down to the end of what you can do. The tip-out, or bay window, you can handle with the help of two friends. After you remove the outside seals and inside finishing strips, the tip-out swings down into the living room on its floor hinges. The same with the bay window. However, half way down, the tip-out gets very heavy, which is the reason you need help for that last few feet to the floor.

Fig. 9-3. The endless accumulation of tools, garden equipment, bicycles, etc., are things you just can't ship in your mobile home. And don't forget about those concrete steps, of which you have three. This is why you must rent a truck.

Expandos can be quite large and weigh half a ton. They must be pushed into the living room on rollers. You will need help for this also. With a tag and a double, you hire specialists who have the necessary hydraulic equipment to raise and move laterally. They will make the separations and fill in the openings with some form of plastic cover or plywood sheets. It is a one-day job and will cost from $200 to $500. It is best not to be around to watch this (Fig. 9-4) because to some it can be a traumatic thing, watching something you love being broken apart.

IS IT CHEAPER TO SELL?

By this time you may be thinking that it would be far simpler to sell your home than move it. It *would* be simpler with some double size homes, like my own, which have been so permanently established, enlarged, and improved because we get carried away and spend more money on improvements and additions than the basic home originally cost. The work of dis-assembling is a staggering job that can take weeks if you have a fulltime job and can only work a few hours each day. If you contract the job, it can cost up to five thousand dollars or more—on *each end*! The total cost for a move can be as high as $12,000, or as low as $600 for a single wide with no additions.

Now, let's look at the selling economics, which I recently did for my own home. My basic home cost $18,000 in 1971. I spent another $12,000 on additions and improvements, for a total of

$30,000. With a little bit of luck, I might be able to sell for about $24,000. However, when I go to replace that same home at *today's* prices, it will cost over $40,000. This represents a paper loss of $16,000.

Doing all of the preparation, dis-assembling, and re-assembling work myself, I could move my home 1,000 miles for less than $2,000. If I contract the work, it will cost 10-12 thousand dollars, which is *still* cheaper than selling.

If I were to sell, the $16,000 loss is *not* tax deductible. You must remember that mobile homes depreciate just like automobiles, while new mobile homes keep increasing in cost. That is the reason for the $16,000 loss. It is depreciation on personal property. That is the reason why you can't sell without losing money. Do most of the preparatory work yourself and you will save money, which is why you bought this book in the first place.

If, in spite of all this, you are still determined to sell rather than move, you will find that mobile homes are something of a paradox in that they are both easy and hard to sell. There is always a big demand for low cost housing, especially one-owner mobile homes less than five years old. A two-liner in the classified ads will have your phone ringing constantly.

What makes mobile homes hard to sell is the obstacle course put in your way by park management. Nothing brings out the tyrant in park owner's quicker than the sight of FOR SALE signs in windows. Immediately royal edicts will go forth through the mails on Xeroxed Proclamations banning forthwith all FOR SALE signs. These will be followed by another royal edict forbidding the use of the park name in any form of advertising.

Many parks are run like baronial fiefdoms of the 15th Century. Some have managers with shaved heads who look like Kojak and have the disposition of Attila the Hun. They have the leverage power to enforce all royal edicts because you can sell your home, but *not* the lot. If your home is not available to a buyer, you have painted yourself into a corner. This is also how the park forces you to pay the "exit" fee when you sell. Either you pay or you are ordered to move your home the instant it is sold. Now, if you move rather than sell, you can tell management where to go for their "exit" fee.

If you are one of those conservative individuals with simple tastes, not easily swept up in the mobile home mania to outdo the neighbors in fancy cabanas, porches, 70-foot enclosed carports, screened patios, and the tallest flagpole, you very wisely bought a

Fig. 9-4. The exposed guts of a mobile home are not a pretty sight, and is probably the biggest reason why so many decide to sell rather than move. If you haven't yet bought a mobile home, just looking at this may save you money if you decide against buying anything that must be put together.

functional 70 × 14 single wide home, with maybe a tip-out or bay window.

You are to be envied, sir. You are a truly free man who can tell Shaved Head park managers to go take a jump. In one day you can have your big, comfortable, adequate mobile home ready for the transport tractor that will move you wherever you want to go and for just a few hundred dollars.

You are to be envied, sir.

10

Saving During The Energy Crisis

When this book was originally conceived, there *was* no energy crisis. Mobile homes were still coming off factory assembly lines with 2 × 3 studding, which makes less space to fill with insulation. New mobile home parks were still being designed and built all over the country with those nostalgic gas postlights in front of every home. Natural gas was still plentiful and cheap and nobody thought it particularly wasteful to have a 24-hour street light burning in front of their home.

But so much has happened in so short a time span that this book would not be complete now without this chapter. There is consternation, even panic, up north in the confused world of mobile homes where the snow falls and the winds blow. When Columbia Gas of Ohio's northwest manager appeared on television with the mayor to announce that contingency plans were being formulated to provide emergency shelter for residential customers who would be forced out of their homes when gas service was curtailed to certain areas, there were two attempted suicides by elderly women living alone in mobile homes.

According to a recent study in California, the elderly are among the most suicide-prone people in the United States. Ray Bourhis, co-director of the Public Interest Law Center, who financed the study, says, "There are 25 million people over 65 in the United States. Most have worked hard all their lives and finally paid off their mortgages, retired, bought a mobile home and now find that they can't afford to pay their heating bills. Like millions of other people, they must choose between buying food or heating fuel."

GAS POSTLIGHT CONTROL

One of the things that amazes me is that the gas company never once asked any of the many mobile home communities to turn off their gas street lights. In my park there are 465. The gas company was too busy, I guess, with the more important business of scaring us all.

I think the gas companies are deeply concerned about the long range impact on their future growth potential. If you ever read the *Wall Street Journal*, you become very familiar with those two words, "growth potential." They mean life or death to a business because without "growth potential" they can't raise capital or borrow money from the banks. If you can't raise capital, you're dead.

I don't think the gas companies really *want* you to turn off your 24-hour gas postlight. A few years ago when average mobile home heating bills during the coldest months were only $20 a month, the added cost of that postlight was trifling. But gas rates have increased *seven times* in just the last year, and heating bills are now averaging $60 a month. That postlight has now become a burden and irritation. What do you do? Should you convert to electricity?

When I first started to write this book, my feelings were that converting to electricity, as I did, was the best deal. But that was before the roof fell in. That was before the utility companies, the petroleum industry and the Arabs took over the world. Converting the postlight to electricity merely increases the size of the check you eventually must mail to the power company. Why not decrease the size of the check you mail to the gas company by installing a gas light control?

This ingenious device is installed right on top of the post, under the lamp housing. It is a three-inch black metal cylinder, about five inches in length, with all the copper fittings necessary for a connection between the gas line and the light. It only takes a few minutes to install and can't be too difficult because a little old lady down the street just installed one all by herself.

The control valve is activated by the same type of photoelectric eye that is used on electric postlights (Fig. 10-1). The gas light is turned up bright at dusk and turned down low in the morning, so low you can see no flame. Actually, it never goes completely out. There is just enough pilot flame to keep it burning.

This control will cut your postlight expenses in half. If a few million mobile homeowners do this, it will cut into the gas company's earnings per share, and this will force them to ask the public utilities commission of your state for another rate increase. Things are tough all over.

The gaslight control costs about forty bucks. Look in the Yellow Pages under "Gaslights." The same people who sell mobile home woodburning fireplaces also sell this item. If they don't have it, try everybody listed under "Gas" in the phone book.

If you decide against installing this control device, think back to last January when the evening television newscasts brought warnings of a possible gas shut-off, and then in the weather report that followed, they told you that temperatures would drop to about 15 below zero.

GAS SHORTAGES

Remember how the gas company never hinted *which* areas might have gas service curtailed? Consequently, everybody worried and waited for the ax to fall, and while they waited they chased all over town buying up all the portable electric heaters, sweaters, thermal underwear and heavy clothing they could find.

It was a great week for business in my area, and one big discount chain sent a truck up into Michigan, where they had no gas shortage, to pick up electric heaters from another outlet in their chain. They brought back 200. They were all gone in less than two hours.

It was a terrible week for the helpless and confused who didn't know how to cope. And some of the dumb things they were told to do only made them more helpless and more confused. TV newscasters would read a list of things people should do if their gas service was cut off.

WHAT NOT TO DO IN A GAS CRISIS

☐ Prepare to evacuate. Take along everything that will be needed to be self sufficient.

☐ Shut off the gas at the meter.

☐ Shut off the water at the main valve.

☐ Flush all toilets.

☐ Blow all water out of pipes with compressed air.

☐ Fill all traps and toilet bowls with anti-freeze.

☐ Drain the hot water tank.

☐ Don't take pets. Leave food and water for them.

☐ Leave door to home unlocked so gas men can enter to retore service, and relight pilot lights.

Fig. 10-1. The gas postlight control valve is activated by a photoelectric eye which turns the gas up at dusk and down in the morning. You can see no flame burning.

The above list of things to do, as silly as some of them are, was repeated over and over in a crisis atmosphere, and it is surprising more elderly people did not commit suicide. The man-made "crisis" is over temporarily, and you can prepare now for the next one. Let's take a long look at each of the items above.

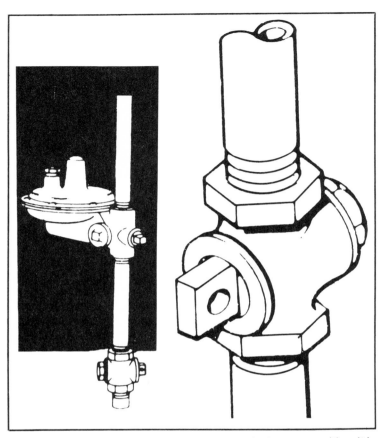

Fig. 10-2. This is the gas shut-off valve. It is now in the open position. It is usually just above ground level before going into the meter.

Prepare To Evacuate. Take Along Everything That Will Be Needed To Be Self-Sufficient. For a family with three children, to be "self sufficient" in some old school buildings set up as an Evacuee Center will require at least two station wagons filled to capacity with mattresses piled on top and looking like something out of the movie, *The Grapes of Wrath*. This is ridiculous. Why should you abandon your home? A gas shut-off is *not* the end of the world. Stay with your home.

Shut Off The Gas At The Meter. Oh sure! It's easy to sit in a TV studio and tell people to shut off their gas, but a lot of people in this world don't know how. The illustration (Fig. 10-2) will show you what the shut-off valve looks like. All it takes is an adjustable wrench or pliers to make a quarter turn on that valve. A small screwdriver inserted in that hole will also work. You may wonder why it is necessary to shut off the gas at the meter since the furnace and water heater both have built-in safety devices which automatically turn off the gas. When gas is again sent into the lines, there will be air to evacuate. There will be pilots to relight.

Shut Off The Water At The Main Valve. This is something else that confuses many women living alone in a mobile home. Where *is* the main shut-off valve for the water?

There are two. One is at the bottom of that hole in the ground, usually under your home, where water service comes to your lot. The pipe from this hole to your home is always covered with heat tape to prevent freezing. At the other end of that heat tape-covered pipe you will find the second shut-off valve. It is always on that same pipe that goes to your outside faucet, the one you use to water the lawn, and it looks like the valve illustrated in Fig. 10-3.

Fig. 10-3. This is the water shut-off valve. It is under the home and on the same water pipe as the outside water faucet.

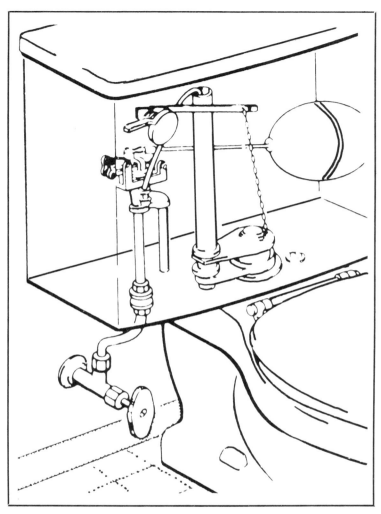

Fig. 10-4. Just screw the connection on the shut-off valve, bottom left, and with a small funnel pour salt water into the piping.

Flush Toilets. This one makes sense because everybody knows how to flush a toilet.

Blow All Water Out Of Pipes With Compressed Air. This one is stupid. Who has a compressor? I am probably the only mobile homeowner in three states who has a compressor, but I am a tool freak. Normal average people just don't own such things. So what do you do? So you open that outside water outlet and, since this is the lowest part of your water system, you hope and pray it all drains out.

There is always the danger that there might be a slight dip in that long length of water line to the front bathroom or kitchen which is in the floor and runs parallel to the heat ducts, which protects it from freezing. To be safe, mix a pitcher of salt water, using table salt. Break the water connection to the front toilet. (It's right under the tank on the left side.) Stick a plastic funnel into the copper tubing and pour in the salt water.

Another way is to break that connection at the bottom of the tank, (Fig. 10-4) pour the salt water into the tank itself and it will all run down the water line and dribble out your outside faucet. When it does, you're safe.

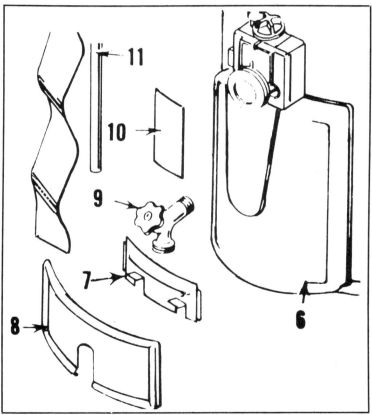

Fig. 10-5. This is the hot water tank drain valve. It is at the very bottom of the tank, and has screw threads for a garden hose so you can drain rust away from your home.

Fill All Traps And Toilets With Anti-Freeze. Oh sure! Doesn't everybody keep anti-freeze around the house for just this purpose? This is another silly one because you don't need anti-freeze. Just plain old kitchen table salt will do just as well. Dump a cup full in the toilet bowls, and two tablespoons into each sink trap and bathtub trap.

Drain The Hot Water Tank. The illustration, (Fig. 10-5) will show you what this drain valve looks like. It is at the very bottom of the tank, and is threaded to take a garden hose so you can drain the rusty water away from your home.

Don't Take Pets. Leave Food And Water For Them. This is a senseless form of cruelty to animals, abandoning them along with your home. They know something is wrong and they won't touch the food you leave for them. They will suffer acutely.

Leave Door To Home Unlocked So Gas Men Can Enter To Restore Service, Relight Pilots. If gas men can get into your home, so can anybody else. This item was the most distressing to many people, not only abandoning their homes and possessions, but leaving it all unprotected with everyone knowing it was open and unprotected. This item you should flush down the toilet, along with most of the others.

SURVIVING WITHOUT GAS

Nobody can force you to abandon your home, your possessions, or your pets. And you can survive without gas, and you will survive a lot better in your own home, much better than you will in some so-called "Evacuee center" with Salvation Army coffee and donuts. The worst part is the morbid sight-seers who drive by in their warm cars to stare at you. I was most distressed by this when I was once flooded out of my home by Lake Erie high waters—the long line of sight-seers driving by on a Sunday afternoon to gawk at my misery.

According to the *Wall Street Journal*, the government has been warned in confidential briefing papers that the natural gas shortage will continue for at least the next two winters. So you might as well start thinking about next winter *now* while you're cutting the grass. Don't be like those people who got screwed last winter when they panic-bought portable electric heaters at suddenly jacked-up prices.

ELECTRIC HEATERS

If you intend to go with electric heaters, buy them in mid-summer at discount prices. I personally will be buying three heavy duty utility electric heaters. They have a suggested retail price of $32.95, and a discount price of $23.27. I will keep these heaters stored away in their original factory boxes unopened. If future natural gas shortages fail to materialize, I can sell the heaters as brand new merchandise and recover my full investment.

Surviving With Electric Heaters

The heavy duty utility electric heaters I am buying have two heat ranges, 1250 and 1500 watts. This translates to 4266 and 5120 BTU's. The letters "BTU" mean British Thermal Unit, the amount of heat required to raise one pound of water one degree Farenheit.

One KWH (kilowatt hour) of electricity will produce the same amount of heat that you would get consuming 10.4 cu.ft. of natural gas or 0.88 lbs. of coal. The average KWH rate that you pay for electricity is roughly about four cents. The way electric companies figure out your bill is very complicated, but if you use four cents as a base computing rate, you will come surprisingly close no matter where you live in the United States. Therefore, if you burn fifteen 100 watt light bulbs for one hour, it will cost you about six cents because you have consumed 1½ KWH's of electricity.

The same thing will apply to any electric heater you buy, whether it is regular or heavy duty. You can expect 5120 BTU's of heat from 1500 watts, no more and no less, and it will cost you approximately six cents an hour. The only reason I am buying "heavy duty" units is because they have a better blower fan and resistor heating elements. There are some very expensive heaters available with more heat ranges, thermostats and chrome trim, but they add nothing to the unit's ultimate usefulness, which is to give you BTU's of heat, which will cost you six cents an hour. As the philosopher said, "All else is vanity."

To figure amperage, divide 1500 watts by 125 volts, and you get 12 amps. For 1250 watts you get 10 amps. Mobile home circuits are wired and fused to handle a 20 amp load but don't push them. Don't *ever* try to put two electric heaters on the same circuit.

If you look at your fuse box in the back bedroom, you will see rows of circuit breaker switches with the number "20" molded on them. Each of those switches represents a different circuit, each can handle a load up to 20 amps before heating up and breaking connection, which is the same as blowing an old fashioned fuse. Your home will have 8, 10, or 12 regular 20 amp circuits depending on the size of your home. You will also have one 30 and one 50 amp circuit. These are for the electric range and air conditioner.

It is a good idea to identify all the regular 20 amp circuits so that you know which in case you replace a wall switch or make other repairs. To identify them, just turn on all your light, throw each circuit breaker to the "off" side, and note which lights in the home go off. Do the same with all the wall outlets by plugging in a table lamp.

With three electric heaters, set one up at each end of the home, one in the center. This will definitely put you on three different circuits. If the center heater is in the kitchen, check to be sure it is not on the same circuit as the kitchen appliance outlet. This is the one near the sink that your wife uses with her toaster and electric skillet. If it is, use an extension cord and plug the heater into another room.

How Warm With Electric Heaters

With three heaters set at the maximum 1500 watt range, costing you 18 cents an hour, your mobile home will be livable but not too warm if it is windy and outside temperatures are near zero. If it is not windy, if the sun is shining and temperatures are above zero, you could be even warm and comfortable. But if you thought of this during the summer and bought thermal underwear, you will survive and be a lot happier then you would be in some "Evacuee Center" eating donuts.

PROTECTING WATER HEATERS FROM FREEZING

Portable electric heaters will take care of your home interior and inside plumbing, and the heat tape will protect the water line, but there is still that uncovered water line to the gas water heater. When in operation, there is enough residual heat from the tank, pilot light and burners to keep the tiny water tank compartment above the freeze level. But with no gas, that exposed water line will freeze.

The easiest way to prevent this is to do something I learned as a boatman. When my cruiser was in winter storage under canvas, a certain amount of rain and snow would blow through ventilation openings and get into the bilges. When water in the bilges freezes, it opens up seams. I couldn't keep the water out, but I could keep it from freezing. I did this with two 100 watt light bulbs burning constantly in the bilge. You would be amazed at the amount of heat put out by an electric light bulb in a small enclosed area. The temperature in my bilge never dropped below 40 degrees, even in the coldest weather, and the heat eliminated sweating, rust and corrosion on the engines. Only thing, the light bulbs must be checked often because they don't last long.

Do the same thing in your water heater compartment. There is a hole in the back wall where the copper plumbing passes through, usually into the bathroom. You can easily pass an electric extension cord through this hole to a 100 watt bulb mounted into porcelain light recepticle and sitting upright on the floor. That one bulb will produce enough heat to save your water heater at a cost of four cents for every 10 hours of burning.

PROTECTING WATER LINES IN THE FLOOR

There is one more problem, and you should prepare for it during good weather. There is that long water line which runs to the front bathroom, or kitchen if you have one here. This line runs parallel with the heat ducts, which keep it from freezing. With the furnace off and no heat passing through that duct, this line could freeze, and if it does, it will be a major disaster. Protect this line at all cost because it is difficult to get at for repair. You'll have to tear up all the floors. It's too horrible to even contemplate.

You can keep this line from freezing by leaving a pencil-thick stream of water running at all times. But, when you do this, you create another monster, the likelihood that this slow trickle of water will freeze in the plastic sewer line under the home. This particular sewer line, whether it's the front bathroom or kitchen, is almost always quite long, sometimes 50 feet, and it has very little drop. Under normal usage, like flushing a toilet, running the garbage disposal or the dishwasher, water just surges through and doesn't stay in the pipe long enough to freeze. But when you have water dribbling through that pipe in a steady unbroken flow, it *will* freeze and create a dam. Water will back up behind the dam and freeze into a solid mass.

PROTECTING THE SEWER LINE FROM FREEZING

In an earlier chapter, I detailed how this particular sewer line could be protected with heat tape in the same manner as your water line from the ground to the home. So wind non-thermostat type heat tape on that sewer line while the weather is pleasant. If your sewer pipe is plastic, do not cover the heat tape with insulation. Put an easy-to-reach switch on the heat tape so you can turn it on and off at will. Remember, this heat tape is on that pipe *only* as an insurance policy, to get you out of trouble in a hurry next winter when it's too cold to be crawling around under the home.

With your front sewer line protected with heat tape you can safely let the water dribble in a pencil-thick flow to keep that floor water line from freezing. Keep all the cupboard doors to bathroom and kitchen sinks open. Even though it's warm in the home, it can get cold under there.

You are now protected from freeze-ups, your home is warm enough to live in, if you dress properly, and you will survive. That is all that matters, surviving at home with your family, and not in some school building set up as an Evacuee Center.

WOODBURNING FIREPLACES

An alternate method of obtaining supplemental heat is the woodburning fireplaces that are made expressly for mobile homes. They are good and will keep you warm and comfortable in one room, even when you have the thermostat lowered to 60 degrees. But they provide no heat for other rooms, even with a circulating fan. In the event of a total gas shut-off, you will still need two electric heaters to keep tempertures above freezing at the rear and front of the home.

Woodburning fireplaces are usually installed in the living room or family room. They will provide more heat than a third electric heater and, if you use the new rolled-up newspaper logs, will be considerably cheaper than electricity or all-wood log burning.

Fireplace Chimneys

Mobile home fireplaces require a hole in the roof for a special type chimney, and another hole in the floor to provide outside oxygen for combustion. The explanation you will get for this is that mobile homes are so well insulated and sealed up that there just isn't enough air in the home to provide good combustion and leave enough oxygen for the occupants.

I find this hard to believe. I have spent days in a tiny wilderness hunting shack with four other men, two dogs and a cast-iron cookstove burning red-hot all the time. There was no shortage of oxygen for the stove or us, and that 12 × 15 wood shack was pretty well sealed up with tar paper.

Anyway, that's what it says in the directions when you buy a woodburning fireplace, and if you have the dealer install it, his men will cut a 10 × 12 hole in your floor to the crawl space below. Incidently, if you have the dealer make the installation, be sure that this hole is covered with window screen material. If you don't, you will go crazy trying to figure out how all the flies and mosquitoes are getting into your home.

Personally, I don't think that hole in the floor is really necessary and I would never have it in my home. For thousands of years, Man has lived with an open fire in his home. In England and Europe, where central heating is a rarity, there is a fireplace in every room. That's why English homes have so many chimneys. In the United States, there are 100 million homes with one or more fireplaces. How do they survive without a square hole in the floor? A friend of mine asked that same question. So he installed a woodburning fireplace in his mobile home without that hole in his floor. So far nobody in his family of five is gasping for air like a goldfish out of water, and the fireplace burns very well.

The Best Wood For Fireplaces

Softwoods like fir, pine, spruce and aspen burn fast and hot. Hardwoods like oak, ash and fruitwood burn slower and with less flame but produce a radiant bed of hot coals. They are the best buy. Only seasoned wood should be used in a fireplace. Green wood produces little heat because most of its energy is used up just consuming itself.

You cannot start a hardwood fire with just a match, and don't mess around with kerosene, fuel oil, or lighter fluid because there is always the danger of unexpected ignition or reverse flashing. Do it the old fashioned way with crumpled up paper and small kindling, gradually working up to larger pieces of wood, small logs on the bottom, big on top. Be sure to keep a safety screen in front of the fireplace.

Rolled-Up Newspaper Logs

There is a device on the market (Fig. 10-6) for making logs for fireplaces out of old newspapers. I have seen it done. I have seen them burn. They give off as much heat as hardwood logs, burn just as long (2-3 hours), burn clean with no objectionable odor, with no snap, pop or unexpected shower of sparks, and they leave little ash. If you like the sound and sentiment of a real log fire, plus the economy of paper logs, you can burn one wood log with three paper logs.

I have learned that the whole secret of good paper logs is rolling them *tight*. The finished log should be 3½ to 4 inches in diameter. Now here's the bad news. It takes about a week's supply of newspaper to make one log, and you will burn it up in about two or three hours. That means you better start rolling up logs in the summer and lay in a good supply and keep them dry.

...*Rolls any Newspaper into Fireplace Logs!*

Fig. 10-6. Start rolling your newspaper logs in midsummer because a week's supply of newspaper makes only one log, which will burn up in about three hours.

If nobody sells this roller in your area, you can buy direct from *Christen, Inc.*, 59 Branch Street, St. Louis, Mo. 63147. And if you decide to go with paper logs and a fireplace, I might as well give you *all* the bad news. The woodburning fireplaces are not cheap. The one my friend had installed cost $550. You can save $100 by installing yourself. Lots of luck.

THE CAST-IRON WOOD/COAL STOVE

These two old relics of the past (Fig. 10-7) are making all the nostalgia freaks happy. Pound for pound, there is no piece of Americana that has served so many so well as these two cast-iron Early American stoves. They both put out a tremendous amount of heat for their size. The box heater model, although not as attractive as a woodburning fireplace, is far more useful because not only will it heat up your entire home, it will cook your meals as well. This stove is still the primary heat and cooking equipment in many sections of the United States, Canada and Alaska.

Since the fire is totally enclosed, you can get either of these stoves red-hot and, with a circulating fan you can heat up a barn. In fact, I actually did this once when I was building a boat in a friend's barn. I worked all winter, often in sub-zero temperatures, and a potbelly stove kept me warm.

If you want the best of all insurance policies against freezing next winter if the gas is shut off, this is *it*. That is if you don't having something in your living room that will clash with the Mediterranean decor. The little cast-iron beasts are not pretty, but they really do a job.

You will, of course, need a chimney. If you never use the stove, it will still make an interesting conversation piece, and a place to hide things, like your expensive Scotch.

Chimney Flue Heat Loss

You have undoubtedly received mail from the hustlers who take advantage of every ill wind. The better parks do not permit

Fig. 10-7. These two Early American cast-iron stoves are making a big comeback right now. The bottom potbelly produces the most heat. The box heater can also be used for cooking.

salesmen or peddlers, but there's always the junk mail route addressed to Occupant. One of the pieces of junk hitting the mailboxes right now is the routine about money going up your chimney flue (Fig. 10-8). This is a much discussed subject right now and controversial with too much pro, too much con. There are vested interests with much to gain. The principle is that the furnace flue updraft not only draws out combustion waste products, it draws out heat as well. When the furnace is in the off cycle, this updraft keeps pulling heat out of your home.

These arguments, convincing as they are, do not apply to mobile home heating systems. Remember that, and don't let anybody con you into spending a great deal of money for something you do *not* need. Your mobile home furnace comes equipped with a special type of chimney with an outer sleeve through which is admitted outside air for combustion. Therefore, your furnace does not draw on the air in your home for combustion, and consequently no heat is wasted by going up the chimney.

You do not need an expensive electronic ignition system to replace your perfectly adequate gas pilot light. The pilot light uses only pennies of gas in a month and it serves a useful purpose other than ignition. In the off season, if you leave it on, it protects your furnace from dampness and rust. Those pennies are cheap insurance.

Beware of Insulation Con Men

Another big mobile home con game right now is the blow-in-insulation-from-the-roof routine. This one is cruel because its primary victims are retirees and old widows who already are having a rough time just surviving. And yet they shell out $1400 for absolutely nothing.

I call this a con game because what they tell you is false, and what they say they will do is impossible. They are either ignorant, stupid or crooked. Have nothing to do with them.

They claim that insulation in your outer walls is either skimpy or non-existent. This is false. They claim that they can correct this without tearing up your home by drilling holes in your roof and then blowing insulation down between the sds. This is impossible!

To understand why this is impossible, take a long look at the skeleton drawing (Fig. 10-4) of a mobile home. The construction detail is typical of all manufacturing methods in the industry. You will note that a mobile home is not framed quite the same as a conventional home. Note the many *horizontal* frames, or stringers,

Fig. 10-8. This type of scare copy is hitting the mobile home mailboxes right now. This is junk mail in more ways than one. Junk it!

and note how the skeleton frame of a mobile home consists of many square closed off sections.

Now, assuming as the salesman tells you, that there is no insulation whatsoever in those square sections, how do you blow insulation in *all the way to the bottom?* How do you blow past those horizontal frames? It's impossible! And another thing, no matter what the salesman says, those square sections in the walls are *not* empty air space. They are *already* filled with fiberglass insulation. So how do you blow anything in there? It's impossible! All they do is blow insulation material into the roof air space. In this respect, you are getting *some* insulation, but not where you think.

In the past six years I have seen a great many mobile homes of different manufacture in various stages of remodeling work. I have

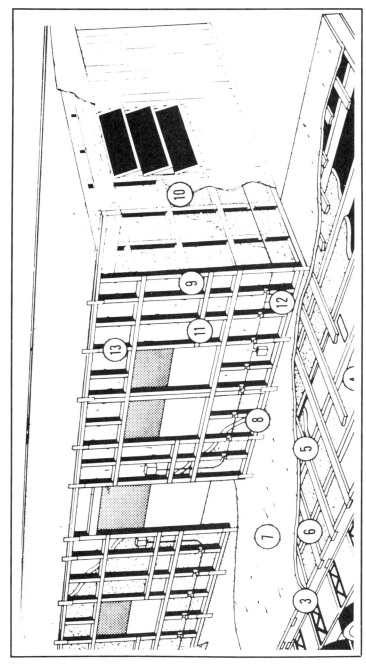

Fig. 10-9. Note all the horizontal stringers in mobile home structural framing. It is impossible to blow insulation down from the roof.

never yet seen one that did not have plenty of fiberglass insulation in the outer walls. I am no friend of the manufacturers. I owe them nothing, and they have given me no help in gathering material for this book. I have no reason to be anything but totally honest in presenting the facts as I, a mobile homeowner myself, see them. There are a great many things that I don't like about mobile homes, but the amount of insulation between the walls is not one of them. So don't let yourself be conned into spending $1400 for something you do not need.

THE BEST AND CHEAPEST INSULATION

One of the oldest and best insulation materials known is that white stuff called snow. People are forever trying to get rid of it whereas up in Canada and Alaska they keep it and use it for insulation. Eskimos even make their homes out of it.

A homeowner in my park demonstrated to me the amazing insulating qualities of snow last winter when outside temperatures dropped to 17 below zero and high winds brought a wind chill factor of 65 below. Many residents in the park, whose homes were situated so they got the wind full broadside, had frozen traps in their bathtubs and frozen hot water lines to their shower heads. Bathtub shower water lines come up between the walls, but it took

Fig. 10-10. This is one man's way of insulating his home and shielding it from prevailing winds, which in January brought a wind/chill factor temperature of 65 below zero.

Fig. 10-11. This type of mobile home is most likely to have a sudden heat bill increase (courtesy Woodall Publishing Co.).

65 below zero to get through to the hot water line. And yet, the cold water line did not freeze. That proves something, there must be some insulation in those walls.

I mention this mainly to illustrate how cold it was that day terrible day, and the fact that this other resident took a thermometer reading of the temperature under his mobile, and it was 36 degrees.

How could this be, with a wind chill factor of 65 below zero? This man insulated with snow, as they do in the Alaskan bush. While everybody else was shoveling snow, throwing it out in the street or piling it up on the sidewalks, this man was throwing the snow up against his home to a height which completely covered his skirting. He did this on all four sides of his home, completely sealing off the crawl space. That did it. That's how Eskimos live, completely surrounded by snow with not even a pinhole left open.

There are many ways to "insulate" to shield your home from wind. You can surround your home with shrubbery. You can do what the man in the illustration did (Fig. 10-10), completely close off the side of the home which faces the prevailing winds of winter. This man reports a 20 percent drop in gas usage—I said *usage*, not dollars. There's a difference. You can reduce your gas usage 50 percent and still pay out the same dollars every month because the cubic foot rate on which you are billed is constantly going up— actually seven times in the last year. If you do not reduce your usage, you will see the difference, as many have who report gas bill increases from $20 a month to $70, $80 and $90 a month.

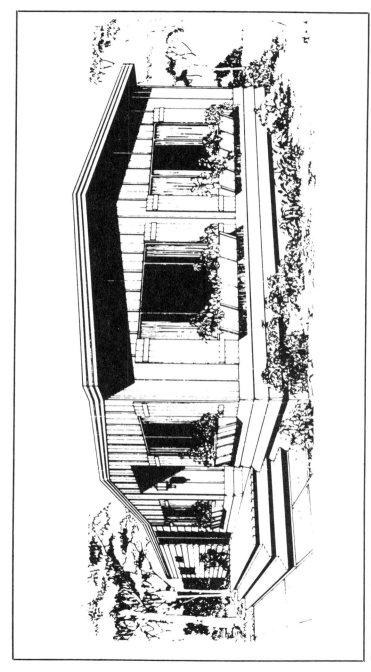

Fig. 10-12. Another type of mobile home which is likely to have sudden heat bill increases (courtesy Woodall Publishing Co.).

TWO BAD HEATING SYSTEMS

Most big gas bill increases are being reported by homeowners who live in two types of mobile homes, the big "tags" and the doubles (Fig. 10-11 and Fig. 10-12). My home is one of those with a big "tag" and I quickly discovered the reason for a sudden big gas bill, as I reported in an earlier chapter.

These two home types have a fundamental weakness in their heat distribution systems, which also applies to air conditioning since it uses the same ducts. The furnace is in one half of the home. Getting heat into the other half is what causes problems.

You would assume, as I once did, that when the two halves are put together, the two duct systems would sort of telescope together and become one distribution system. That isn't the way it is at all. Long flexible ducts, about 15 inches in diameter, are used under the home to move heat from the furnace to the ducts in the "tag" or other half of the double.

I have witnessed the installation of these flexible ducts a hundred times, and it is always done by boys who don't like this particular chore. They're always in a hurry to finish, and as a result this most important work on your heating system is done haphazardly and hurriedly by kids who just want to get out from under your home. I am not exaggerating, I have seen this too many times.

If you find your flexible ducts just half-hanging to the furnace pipe nipple by a strip of dried-out aluminum duct tape, that is the reason your gas usage suddenly zoomed. You are heating the crawl space.

A good idea given to me by a mobile homeowner was to install one of those remote type indoor-outdoor thermometers with the long cable attached to a sending unit. The sending unit you install under your home; the thermometer you mount in your home. This makes it easy to constantly monitor temperatures in the crawl space. If it suddenly gets warm down there, you know there's a leak somewhere.

Think of all these things now, and not next winter when they threaten you with another gas shut-off and higher fuel bills. It will keep you out of those Evacuation Centers. I've been there once. The coffee's terrible. No matter how rough it gets, stay with your home.

And good luck.

Index

224

Edited by Steven H. Mesner